101

Amusing

Ways to Develop
Your Child's

Thinking
Skills

and

Creativity

101
Amusing Ways to Develop Your Child's Thinking Skills and Creativity

by

Sarina Simon

UPDATED EDITION
Updated by Oksana Hlodan

Lowell House
Los Angeles

Contemporary Books
Chicago

Library of Congress Cataloging in Publication Data

Simon, Sarina.
    101 amusing ways to develop your child's thinking skills and creativity.

    "For Preschool–Third Grade"
    1. Educational games.   2. Thought and thinking—Study and teaching (Preschool)   3. Creative activities and seat work. 4. Education, preschool—Parent participation.   I. Title. II. Title: One hundred one amusing ways to develop your child's thinking skills and creativity.   III. Title: One hundred and one ways to develop your child's thinking skills and creativity.
    LB1140.35.E36S55   1989   371.3'9   89-2796
    ISBN 0-929923-03-0
    ISBN 1-56565-479-X (updated edition)

Requests for such permissions should be addressed to:
Lowell House
2020 Avenue of the Stars, Suite 300
Los Angeles, CA 90067

Lowell House books can be purchased at special discounts when ordered in bulk for premiums and special sales. Contact Department TC at the address above.

Publisher: Jack Artenstein
Associate Publisher, Lowell House Adult: Bud Sperry
Managing Editor: Maria Magallanes
Text design: Laurie Young

Manufactured in the United States of America
10 9 8 7 6 5 4 3 2 1

To Morgan and Nina—
sources of endless delight and inspiration

Contents

Introduction to the Updated Edition   1

How This Book Is Organized   3

Materials to Have on Hand   4

Logic and Classification   7

Picture Battleship   9

True or False   10

Patterns   11

Light & Shadow   12

Feely Boxes   13

The Witch's Diet   15

Try to Remember   15

What Am I?   16

Back Seat Farmers   17

Under the Blanket   18

Bark, Doggie, Bark   19

Landlubbers and Pirates   20

Supermarket Riddles   21

I Went to Town   22

Out of Sight   23

Cupboard Categories   24

I Can't Believe I Forgot Already! 25

Right, Left, or Straight? 25

What's New? 26

Boxing Match 27

Twisters 28

Pair Off 29

African Tic-Tac-Toe 30

Marshmallow 32

Memory Mystery 33

Moving Time Line 34

Concept Capers 35

Nature's Memory Challenge 37

The Art of the Picture Puzzle 38

Reading and Language Arts 41

Movie Time 42

Half a Letter 44

A Colorful Tale 45

Category Bingo 46

Balloon Friend 47

ABC Sillies 49

Giant Wordsearch 50

Softer-Louder 51

Face to Face 52

Alphabet Scavenger Hunt 53

Who Am I? 55

I Can Read!   56

Stepping Stone Game   57

Secret Sounds   58

Tee Shirt Phonics   59

Highway Colors   61

Roadside Alphabet   62

What's in a Name?   63

Decoder   64

Word for a Day   65

The Thanksgiving Tradition Touch*   66

Invisible Ink   68

Math   69

Tic-Tac-Toe-Twelve   71

Plus & Minus Cards   72

Mystery Number   73

Multiplying Mirrors   74

License Plates   75

Clock Game   76

Guesstimating   78

Knock 'Em Down, Add 'Em Up   79

The Long and Short of It   80

Small, Medium, Large   81

Odd or Even?   82

Snake Eye   84

*Holiday Activities

A-Marketing We Will Go 86

Shape Builders 87

Addition Magician 88

Contortion 90

Survey 92

Shape Toss 93

Fivepenny Morris 95

Gelatin Giggles 96

Cranberries and Popcorn—A Chain for Your Christmas Tree* 98

A Weighty Question 99

Television Tally 100

Christmas or Chanukah Calendar* 102

Science and Social Studies 105

Sounds Good 107

Piñata Wishes 108

Over the Rainbow 110

Carrot Plant 111

Bath Boat 112

Heat Conductors 114

Seeing Stars 115

Why Milk? 116

Patriotic Flowers* 117

Butterflies Are Free 119

Full of Air 120

Salty Crystals 121

*Holiday Activities

Fossil Foolery   122

How Does Your Garden Grow?   124

An Herb Garden—Egg Carton Style   125

Wild Bird Feeder   127

Autumn Placemats   128

Rainy Day Fun   130

Hug a Tree   132

The World by the Tail   133

People and Places in Your Neighborhood   134

Motor Development and Self-Awareness   137

Stackable Castle   139

Skittle Bowling   140

My Personal Crest   141

My Community   142

Basketball Star   144

Kick It   145

Finger Lickin' Good   146

One in a Million   147

Chopstick Race   148

Shades of the Past—Making Silhouettes   149

Self-Portrait   150

Makeup Mirrors   151

At the Hop   152

Paper Doll Capers   154

Shadow Drama   155
Obstacle Fun   156
First Up   157
Winter Count   158
"Formal" Dining   160

Art and Creativity   163
Squeeze It   165
Ex Libris   166
Crayon Etchings   167
Cobweb Ball   168
Bubble Art   169
Tablecloth Art   170
Junior Architect   172
Paint-a-Cookie   173
Bath Beautification   175
She Saves Seashells   176
Sponge Printing   177
Soap on a Rope   178
Play Clay   180
Rainy Day Scrapbook   181
Stamp Treasure Box   182
Snowscaping   184
Holiday Magnets*   185

*Holiday Activities

Introduction
to the
Updated Edition

Most parents are busy trying to balance the demands of children, homemaking, and work. Sometimes this can be a challenge. It isn't easy to sandwich quality time between broken washing machines, deadlines, carpools, and dinners. Still, we all agree that no matter how important our other responsibilities are, our number one priority is our children. You may have discovered that you don't have to spend all of your available time at home helping your child learn. What's crucial is providing them with a special time that is reserved only for them, at least once a day.

We often think that schooling will take care of much of our children's education. What children need most is the understanding that learning is a valuable life-long process, and you are the ideal role model for this. Your example will show your children that learning is fun, challenging, and rewarding. Share your own experiences and dreams with your children. Talk about your own feelings and expectations. Encourage them to ask you questions about your beliefs, goals, and actions.

This book is for parents who want to make the most of the time devoted to their children. It is for parents who want to play an active role in the growth of a child into a happy, productive individual. The activities suggested in each of the sections approach learning as a fun experience. They do not demand rote memorization of facts but rather the acquisition of thinking skills and creative processes. The world is full of ever-changing facts. How you arrive at them and what you do with them is what counts in personal growth and achievement.

The 101 activities in this book are easy to implement and require little or no preparation or materials. This updated edition also includes additional activities and extensions, all of which will help you turn your children's world into a learning laboratory—a place where, with your guidance, they can experiment, hypothesize, and make discoveries wherever they go.

How This Book Is Organized

The Book
This book is divided into six sections:

> Logic and Classification
> Reading and Language Arts
> Math
> Science and Social Studies
> Motor Development and Self-Awareness
> Art and Creativity

These areas were chosen because they all contribute in some way to your child's overall intellectual, emotional, and social development. Naturally, there is some overlap between sections. Many activities have extension portions which expand them well beyond their original scope.

The Activities
Each activity includes the following information:

- How long the activity will take. (A plus sign after the time symbol indicates that the activity could extend well beyond the initial time period if you want it to.)
- A list of the materials you will need. (These are almost always simple "around the house" supplies.)

◎ Step-by-step instructions for implementing the activity.

◎ An extension activity to expand upon the basic concept introduced in the activity. If you have time to use the extensions, they provide you with additional 101 activities to share with your children.

◎ Most activities require only you and your child. When an activity is designed for more than two people, the total number of players is stated in the materials list.

Holiday Activities

A few activities in this book are designed to be used at holiday time. You will find them indicated by a special symbol in the table of contents.

Materials to Have on Hand

Many of the activities in this book require simple supplies that we suggest you keep on hand. Many times a boring "there's nothing to do" day can be transformed by a well-stocked supply cupboard.

> Assorted paint (powder, liquid, etc.)
> Assorted paper of different colors and sizes (tissue, construction, newsprint, etc.)
> Balloons
> Drinking straws
> Boxes—clean, empty, sturdy (oatmeal containers and others)

Cardboard tubes
Cellophane tape
Child-size scissors
Clay
Crayons
Fabric scraps
Felt tip markers
Foil
Glitter
Index cards
Masking tape
Paintbrushes, assorted sizes
Painting apron (an old shirt will do)
Paper clips
Pasta (various fun shapes)
Plastic bottles
Play dough
Popsicle sticks
Ruler
Rubber bands
Spools of thread (keep the empty ones, too)
Stickers (teacher supply stores seem to stock the
    least expensive ones)
String
Tape measure
Toothpicks
White craft glue
Yarn

—and *never* throw away a large appliance box without considering what kind of grand fort, castle, or hideaway it might become!

Logic and

Classification

T he thinking games in this section are designed for children to have fun while they exercise their reasoning powers. Research shows that even a few hours a week performing thinking activities improves a child's performance and development. Most methods for the development of thinking skills stress the same thing: there is more than one way to look at things and different ways to arrive at a conclusion. The process is more important than the result.

Challenge your children to be adventurous and creative in their thinking:

- Urge them to examine information from many different viewpoints.
- Ask them to look for connections.
- Allow them to form opinions.
- Above all, talk about the process they took along the way from perception to conclusion.

Whether you're a fan of the philosophy "I think, therefore I am," or the theory "I act, therefore, I am,"—you realize the importance of thinking skills to your well-being. Don't underestimate the power of puzzles, games, and mind benders in your child's growth. Try an adventure game on the computer with your child. See how far you and your child get with a board game that demands strategy. And the simplest of all, ask your child to imagine "What if?" scenarios during the day's ordinary routines.

Picture Battleship

½ to ¾ hour

This game is based on the popular board game "Battleship." It requires the skills of identification, estimating, classification, and organization.

Supplies

Paper or index cards

Markers or crayons

Two or more players

Directions

Draw 5 by 5 grids on two pieces of paper for each player. Label the top rows with the letters A through E and mark the numbers 1 through 5 down the left-hand side. Choose a simple category for each game, e.g., animals, vegetables, fruits, furniture. Each player secretly draws a picture for the chosen category in a square on one of his/her grids. For example, if the category is furniture, the child might draw a chair or a lamp. The grid with the illustration is held out of sight of other players. The second, empty grid is placed on the table in front of the player. Players take turns asking each other about the location of pictures on the grids. For example, "Does your picture cover square A-3?" If the answer is "yes," the player who guessed correctly blackens that square on his/her blank grid with a marker. The player with the most blackened squares wins.

Extension

Add the challenge of risk taking by allowing players to guess what the pictures are at any point in the game. If a guess is wrong, the player loses a turn to ask a question during the game. If the guess is correct, the player automatically wins the game.

True or False

½ to 1 hour

When you are told something, a complex sequence of thinking skills comes into play—from imagery to classification. Can your child recognize the truth in a statement? This logic game is especially fun when a lot of people are visiting your home.

Supplies

> Index cards
> Markers or crayons
> Pictures from printed material, e.g., magazines, catalogues
> Glue
> Two to twenty players

Directions

Draw or paste pictures on index cards. Here are some suggestions for images: flashlight, cup, pail, book, clock, stamp, car, cat, dog, telephone, guitar, toaster, chair, tree, flower. Players form two teams. Each player has one or more picture cards. Players from opposing teams take turns by showing one card at a time and making a statement about the object on their card that is either true or false. Team A must either agree with the statement made by Team B or correct it and vice versa. When a player does not correctly recognize a statement as true or false, he/she loses a card to the opposing team. The team that collects the most cards wins.

Extension

This game can be made more difficult in the following way: teams must give statements that are opposite in truth or falsity to each other's. If Tom, for example, in Team A gives a correct statement and Jenny, for example, in Team B agrees, then Jenny must give a false statement about her picture. If Tom gives an incorrect statement and Jenny corrects him, then she must provide a correct statement about her picture when it's her turn to play.

Patterns

½ hour +

A pattern means repetition, whether it's a shape, line, color, texture, or other element that is repeated. The repetition is rhythmical, just like the note and pause in music. Creating patterns will call on logic skills and perception.

Supplies

Paper clips
Pennies
Construction paper

Directions

Your child will use paper clips or pennies or both to create designs, starting from a simple design with a few pennies to a more complicated one that combines many clips and pennies. Begin by asking your child to place only a few pennies on a sheet of paper to make a pattern. Some children will confuse a design with a pattern. Explain that random placement of objects does not make a pattern. Illustrate a pattern if necessary by looking at household objects, for example, patterned paper towels, wallpaper, wrapping paper, items of clothing. After talking about what you have discovered, increase the number of pennies for more patterns. You can then go on to a combination of pennies and paper clips to make patterns.

Extension

Create wrapping paper with pattern designs for different occasions: birthdays, Halloween, Valentine's Day, etc. Your child can use markers and pre-cut shapes to make the paper.

Light & Shadow

¼ to ½ hour

Perspective is not an easy concept for a child to learn. One of the simplest ways to introduce a child to perspective (distance and scale) is to play with the shadows that objects create.

Supplies

Several small objects (e.g., mug, can, picture frame)
Light-colored table (or a table covered by a light tablecloth)
Flashlight

Directions

Create an interesting arrangement of objects on a table top. Close the blinds or dim the lights. Shine a flashlight to create interesting shadows on the arrangement. Shine it from different angles and distances. Talk about the shadows created. Which shadows are longer? Shorter? Clearer? Why?

Extension

Play a shadow game. Collect small everyday objects such as a mug, toy, keys, or leaf. Take turns with your child to sit on a chair facing a wall. Switch on a flashlight and darken the room. The person who is the quiz master stands behind the seated person, shines the light on the wall, and holds one object in front of the light so that its shadow falls on the wall. With practice, you will learn how to hold the object in such a way that its shadow is not easy to recognize.

Feely Boxes

½ to 1 hour

We usually recognize objects by sight. When you use only your sense of touch, object recognition is not that easy. But it can be loads of fun.

Supplies

Shoe boxes

Masking tape

Scissors or knife

Small objects, e.g., leaves, rice

Directions

Cut a hole in the lid of the shoe boxes so that a hand can fit in easily. Fill each shoe box half full with an object. The contents must be a secret, so you may want to divide the boxes between you and your child. Some suggestions for contents are: sand, marbles, leaves, shredded newspaper, cotton balls, rice, confetti, pasta, dried beans or peas, jelly beans. Caution: none of the objects should have a sharp edge. Tape the lids shut. Put your hand through the hole and feel the texture of the object inside. Can you guess what the object is without peeking?

Extension

Build your child's vocabulary while playing the game. Say words out loud that describe the textures and shapes, e.g., smooth, silky, tiny, cold. When all the objects have been revealed, compare the objects. Which are smooth? Rough? Round? Shiny? etc. You can play this game over and over again, using different objects. You can invite friends to join in the game, too.

The Witch's Diet

½ hour

The best kind of activity: no supplies, no preparation, lots of brain work. This one fills the bill while enhancing language arts skills and creative thinking. It is also a terrific travel game.

Supplies

None

Directions

You begin this alphabetical order game by stating, "The witch is on a diet and she can only eat apples." Next your child must fill in the sentence with a food that starts with letter B: "The witch is on a diet and she can only eat bread." And so on.

Extension

If your child gets stuck on tough letters like Q or Z, show him how to use adjectives, such as "queer cakes" or "a zillion gumdrops. Encourage "language loopholes" like this— it makes the game much more fun.

Try to Remember

¼ to ½ hour

It takes exercise to keep a good memory in shape. Everyone in the family can work out with this observation game.

Supplies

Photos or pictures in books or magazines

Directions

Select a large picture of a scene. Now show your child the picture. Tell her that after she looks at it carefully for a few minutes you will take it away and ask questions to see how much she can remember. Give her three minutes to study the picture. Then, holding the picture so that she cannot see it, ask questions. "What color is the girl's dress? How many people are sitting? Standing? What color is the car? What's the weather?" Give your child a turn to choose a picture and ask you questions.

Extension

Occasionally throw in a question that calls for comprehension instead of just recall. For example, if someone is running to catch a bus, you might ask, "Will someone be late today? How did you know?"

What Am I?

¼ to 1 hour

Improve your child's deductive reasoning skills with this entertaining version of Twenty Questions.

Supplies

Pictures of animals cut out of magazines, newspapers, or drawn on index cards

Tape

Directions

Without letting your child see, take one picture of one animal and tape it to his back. He now asks you (or any other player) questions to find out which animal he is. He can only ask questions that are answered with *yes, no, or sometimes*. Take turns with your child.

Extension

You can also play this game with pictures of objects or photos of friends and family.

Back Seat Farmers

½ hour +

Travel games have always been strong on thinking skills; your brain is about all you can use when you're in a car! Here's one that sharpens visual discrimination, math, and categorizing skills.

Supplies

Car
Pencil and paper
Two players (can also be played in teams)

Directions

Two players sit on opposite sides of the car. One watches the left side of the road, the other watches the right. Each player scores one point for each horse, cow, lamb, dog, cat, or other farm animal that he points out. If he observes an entire group or herd of animals, the player gets ten points.

One person should keep score. Continue until you reach a previously agreed upon score or town.

Extension
If there are not enough players for a real game, your child will still enjoy calling and counting. See how long it takes him to get to 25 points. This game can also be played by counting other things such as roadside restaurants, gas stations, or road signs.

Under the Blanket

½ hour

Perfect for picnic or park days, this activity is suitable for all ages. Your child will get a bit of nature study along with practice in memory and visual discrimination skills.

Supplies
> Blanket or large towel
> Miscellaneous outdoor items (twigs, rocks, acorns, leaves, flowers, and so on)

Directions
Gather five to ten items and spread them out on the bottom half of the blanket. Cover the items with the top half of the blanket. Call your child over and explain that you are going to let him look under the blanket for thirty seconds. Explain that he will see several things that he will be able to find nearby. He should concentrate hard and try to remember all

the items. Then cover the items and give him five minutes to find as many as he can.

Extension

You can play this game indoors, too. If it seems too easy, add more items. If it's too hard, use no more than five.

Bark, Doggie, Bark

¼ to ½ hour

This is a party game that children as young as two can play. It develops auditory discrimination and memory skills—and children adore it!

Supplies
Blindfold

Directions

Have children form a circle. One child is "It" and goes to the center, wearing a blindfold. "It" spins around three times. When she stops, she points to another child in the circle and calls out, "Bark, doggie, bark!" The other child barks like a dog and "It" must guess the identity of the doggie. If "It" is wrong, she changes places with the doggie. If correct, she goes again.

Extension

Vary this game by using different animals and their sounds (e.g., "Moo, Cow, Moo"). Here's another variation: "It" points and asks, "Who are you?" The child in the circle answers,

"My name is_____," giving her real name or someone else's. "It" will have to figure out if the child is telling the truth. If she thinks so, she says "I believe you." If she thinks the child is lying, she says, "Silly, silly, you are_____," giving the correct name.

Landlubbers and Pirates

½ hour

All family members can stretch their classification skills with this super-easy game. Ahoy!

Supplies

One coin

Directions

Flip the coin. If it lands on "heads," call out "Pirates!" If it comes up "tails," call out "Landlubbers!" If you call "Pirates," your child must name an animal that lives in the water. If you call "Landlubbers," he must name a creature that lives on land. Now let your child flip the coin and you name the animals.

Extension

You can play this game with any two categories. Try tame and wild, hot places and cold places, or old things and new things.

Supermarket Riddles

½ to 1 hour

Parents with young children often find trips to the super-market frustrating, but with a little advance planning, shopping excursions can be enormously educational. Here's a mystery game that will develop your child's thinking skills and fill your shopping cart at the same time.

Supplies

Shopping list

Directions

Explain to your child that you are going to play a riddle game. Start in a particular section of the market such as the fruit section. Consult your list and make up a simple riddle such as, "I am red and crunchy. What am I?" If your child cannot guess, add some extra clues such as, "You bob for me on Halloween," or "I am next to the oranges." When your child guesses the item, tell her how many you want and let her help you count them as you place them in your cart. Other riddles might be:

"I make you cry when you peel me."
"I am long and yellow and monkeys like to eat me."
"I am purple and I have the word 'egg' in my name."

Extension

Supermarkets are splendid places for practicing categorization skills. As you walk along the supermarket aisles, ask your child to look carefully at how items are arranged. What would your child call each aisle? Help her identify the dairy section, the frozen food section, the nonfood items, the bakery items, etc. Name some foods and nonfood items and ask your child to guess where they can be found.

I Went To Town

¼ to ½ hour

This variation on the classic game, Grandmother's Trunk, is a triple-header: it combines dramatic skills with memory and motor coordination skills.

Supplies

   None

Directions

Begin by saying, "I went to town and I bought a hat." Pantomime the word "hat" by tipping your hat. Your child goes next, saying, "I went to town and I bought a (she doesn't say the word hat, just pantomimes it) and some soap." She pantomimes soap by pretending to wash. You continue, now pantomiming hat and soap and then adding a new item. This continues until one of you misses. Here are some items that make good pantomime ideas: telephone, dog, comb, toothbrush, ice cream cone, lipstick, powder, pants. This game is terrific for parties, too.

Extension

Play the same way, but this time say, "I went to the zoo (or farm) and saw a _____."

Out of Sight

¼ to ¾ hour

This game is excellent for refining your child's sense of touch and also helps develop his powers of deduction. It's a great parent-child activity but it works equally well with two children.

Supplies

> Two each of small household objects such as paper clips, scissors, toothbrushes, hairbrushes, spoons, etc.
> Two brown paper bags
> Two players

Directions

Put one of each object in each of the bags. Give one bag to each player. Player number one takes an object out of his bag and shows it to the other child. The second child must reach into his bag and, without looking, find the matching object. Players take turns until all the objects are drawn.

Extension

Place one household object in a bag without your child seeing what it is. Have him feel inside the bag and guess what the item is. Continue with remaining objects and then allow him to choose some mystery objects for you to identify.

Cupboard Categories

1 hour +

Categorization is a critical thinking skill. Without the ability to put things into categories, children cannot organize and process information. Here's a simple activity that can improve your child's categorization skills and stock your kitchen cabinets.

Supplies

Groceries to unload from the market

Kitchen

Directions

Take your child with you to the supermarket and point out how items are organized into categories. As you shop, name familiar items and ask her to guess where they might be located. After you return home, have your child help you unload the groceries and place the items into categories on your kitchen table or counter. Ask her where each group of items might belong in your kitchen. Put items away accordingly.

Extension

Examine your cupboards with your child. Are the canned goods in logical groups? How are the pots and pans organized? If you're willing to do a little reorganization (and who among us doesn't need to?), plan out a scheme with her. If your child can print, you might even help her print and decorate labels for some of the shelves and drawers.

I Can't Believe I Forgot Already

½ hour

Keep this in your repertoire for an instant memory and concentration boost—and a lot of fun.

Supplies

None

Directions

Tell your child to look around the room carefully. Have your child close her eyes and ask her simple questions about the room you are in. For example: "What color are the walls? What's on the ceiling? Are there pictures on the wall? How many?" Take turns with your child. You will be surprised at how much you forget, even in the most familiar surroundings.

Extension

This game works well in a waiting room or restaurant. The whole family can join in.

Right, Left, or Straight?

¼ hour +

Young children love to sit in the (figurative) driver's seat. Have your child try this activity to practice visual coordination and test his memory.

Supplies

None

Directions

Make a short road trip via a route that you use regularly—
to the supermarket, the drugstore, the day care center.
Explain to your child that he is going to tell you which way
to drive today. Let him give you directions—right, straight,
etc. Be willing to go the wrong way or continue going
straight if he forgets to tell you to turn. This activity works
best on a Sunday morning when there is a lot of time and
little traffic.

Extension

As you drive your regular routes, have your child continue
to do some navigation. Say, "I'm almost at the Giant Store.
Which way do I turn when I get there?"

What's New?

½ hour

With this simple game your child can markedly increase his
ability to distinguish subtle changes. This activity sharpens
skills of concentration and visual memory for the entire
family.

Supplies

None

Directions

Instruct your child to look at you very carefully. Make sure this includes the front and the back of you, head to toe. Explain that in a few minutes you will leave the room and change something about you. When you return, he will have to say what it is that is now different. When you first play, make the changes obvious; for example, put your hair up or change your shirt. As the game progresses, make the changes more subtle and difficult to detect; for example, change one sock or switch your bracelet to another wrist. Take turns being the observer and the "changer."

Extension

You can play the same observation/memory game with inanimate objects. The observer looks at everything in the room and then leaves for sixty seconds. The "changer" quickly rearranges something in the room.

Boxing Match

½ hour

This match only involves *mental* wrestling! It reinforces the higher-level thinking skill of categorizing.

Supplies

> Index cards
> One shoe box
> Kitchen timer
> Pencil
> Paper

Directions

On ten to twenty index cards write the name of an object or theme such as a gas station, Christmas, camping, kitchen, Halloween, school, supermarket, etc. Shuffle the cards and put them into the box. Read her the card and explain that now she is to name as many things as she can that relate to the word on the card. Set the kitchen timer for five minutes and don't forget to score with pencil and paper. Now you take a turn!

Extension

After your child picks a card, have her cut out pictures of related items from old magazines. She may even want to use construction paper and glue to make a permanent collage.

Twisters

¼ to 1 hour

Tongue twisters are fun and a great way to practice concentration.

Supplies

Watch with a second hand
Two or more players

Directions

Take turns saying each tongue twister three times—as quickly as possible. Here are some classics to start with:

The bank book blew back.
Three terrible thieves.
She sells seashells.
The girl with the green, gray geese.

Time each player to see who can say each twister the fastest with the fewest (or no) mistakes.

Extension

It's even more fun to make up your own tongue twisters. Here are some sounds that make good ones: Th followed by S or T; Z and J; Sw and Sm; Bl and Br; Ch and Cl.

Pair Off

¼ hour

Here's an enjoyable way to stretch memory and classification skills.

Supplies

Common pairs that belong together, such as:

> Cup and saucer
> Knife and fork
> Peanut butter and jelly
> Needle and thread
> Pencil and paper
> Shoe and sock
> Hammer and nail
> Bread and butter

Directions

Mix up all the items and spread them out on a table. Have your child match up the pairs. If that's too hard, try using only six items (three pairs) at a time. If it's too easy, use a kitchen timer and see how many pairs your child can match in three minutes.

Extension

Turn this activity into an exciting scavenger hunt that one or more children will enjoy. Assemble the pairs and then hide one item from each pair. Give a time limit and see how many items your child can find and match.

African Tic-Tac-Toe

¼ to 1 hour

This African variation on a familiar favorite is an excellent game for developing logic and strategic thinking skills. It's a bit more challenging than the American version but, like its Western cousin, it requires few materials.

Supplies

> Paper and pencil
> Coins or other small objects to use as markers
> Two players

Directions

Draw a grid on a piece of paper. Make the grid large enough to accommodate the markers. The markers will be placed on the intersecting, numbered points. Each player needs three markers. The markers must be easily distinguishable—for example, one player might use dimes while the other player might use pennies.

To play, players take turns placing their markers on intersecting points. The goal is to place three markers in a row. If all the markers are placed without a winner, players take turns moving their markers along the lines one space at a time. The game ends when one player succeeds in positioning three markers in a row.

As you teach this game to your child, be sure to provide tips on how to think ahead and plan game-winning moves. Planning and predicting are two important skills he can gain from this engrossing game.

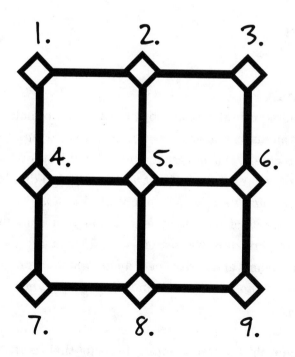

Extension

Create a more complex version of this game by drawing a three box by three box grid. The goal in this version is to place four markers in a row. (Obviously, each player will need four markers, too.)

Marshmallow

½ hour +

This is a great game to play on long car or plane trips. Despite the high calorie name, it's also sugar free! Any way you slice it, Marshmallow sharpens deductive reasoning and inference skills.

Supplies

None

Directions

One person thinks of an object. The person makes statements about that object, substituting the word *marshmallow* for the object. Players try to guess the object. For younger players, keep it easy: "*Marshmallows* like to dig. I always take my *marshmallow* out for a walk. *Marshmallows* bark." The first player makes statements one at a time, until the other players know the secret word. You can also use words that are nouns and verbs: "I got a *marshmallow* on my hand. You *marshmallow* my back and I'll *marshmallow* yours."

Extension

Younger children may enjoy choosing their own "marshmallow" word to use. Older children can play a more sophisticated version of this game by assigning diminishing point values to their clues (for example, first clue, six points; second clue, five points; etc.) and keeping track of their scores.

Memory Mystery

½ hour

A good memory is an important asset. Luckily, memory skills can be honed through practice. Here's a game that's so much fun no one will ever know it's educational.

Supplies
Group of children

Directions
Seat the children in a circle. Choose one child to be "It." Tell "It" to look carefully at the group of children. If necessary, have "It" describe and name each child. Next, tell "It" to close his eyes. Pick one child in the circle to leave the room. Ask "It" to look at the circle and name the missing child. If "It" guesses correctly, he goes again. If not, the missing child becomes "It." Limit the number of times a child can be "It" to two consecutive turns.

Extension
If your group of children finds this game easy, try one of these challenging variations:

1. When "It" hides his eyes, have someone leave the circle *and* have the rest of the children change places in the circle.

2. Arrange the children in the circle so that some are sitting and some are standing. When "It" leaves, ask a standing child to sit and a sitting child to stand. "It" must tell who changed position and how.

3. Have each child hold an object and when "It" leaves the room two children exchange their objects. When "It" returns, she must tell who changed objects.

Moving Time Line

½ hour

Chances are that most children have moved at least once by the time they reach eight or nine years old. Moving can be a traumatic experience but it doesn't have to be. Here's a way to encourage children to share and explore their feelings about moving and, at the same time, develop their classification and sorting skills.

Supplies

Snapshots or drawings of former residences and present home
Any other photos or souvenirs that apply
Roll of white freezer paper, or construction paper taped together
Glue
Markers

Directions

Sort the photos and souvenirs according to the residence(s).

Help your child create a collage-type time line that shows each place he has lived. If possible, include pictures of friends and events that took place at each site. Older children may enjoy making a more elaborate project, perhaps using stick-on letters and numbers for names and dates.

As you work together, talk about what you are doing and what you remember about each home. Encourage your child to talk about his memories—the people, the places, the pets, etc. You may find you derive as much benefit from this activity as does your child.

Extension

Ask your child the following question: "Where do you think you'll be living when you are twenty, forty, sixty?" Ask your child to draw or cut out pictures to show what these places will look like.

Concept Capers

½ hour +

Category information is an important part of learning. In this activity, your child will use inductive and deductive reasoning skills to create and guess categories. This activity takes a little bit of advance preparation but the results are well worth it.

Supplies

Household objects
Magazines that can be cut up

Direction

Choose four or five household items that all belong to the same category—for example, a spatula, a slotted spoon, poultry shears, and a bowl scraper. Place the items before your child and say, "These things are a group. Why do you think I put them all into the same group?" If your child has trouble coming up with an answer, add another kitchen tool and say, "This thing also belongs in this group. Why do you think I put all these things together?" Now, show your child a hammer and say, "This does not belong in the group. Do you know why?" Keep asking questions and adding items until your child identifies the group as the "kitchen tool group." (These exact words are not necessary; a four-year-old might just as well call it the "kitchen cooker things group." It's the concept, not the wording, that matters.)

Try this activity with different groups of items. Use the magazines to cut out pictures of things that can be grouped into categories, for example, things that go, things that fly, happy people, old people, animals with fur, tall buildings, red things.

Extension

Reverse this activity by naming a category and asking your child to find items or pictures that fit into it. Some appropriate categories might be: things to sit on, things to eat with a spoon, things you use in the winter.

If you find your child is good at this exercise, challenge him further by asking him to divide his categories into subcategories. For example, things to eat with a spoon could be divided into things that are generally served hot and things that are generally served cold.

Nature's Memory Challenge

¼ to ½ hour

Another variation on the game Grandmother's Trunk, this is an excellent vehicle for improving concentration and memory skills. In this outdoor version, children develop their memories as they become more aware of the differences between natural and people-made objects.

Supplies

Two or more players

Directions

Two players sit outdoors or look outside a window. The first player names an object that he sees. The object cannot be people-made. (If your child needs help distinguishing between people-made and natural items, explain that people-made objects are things that are made by people such as buildings, pipes, electric wires, etc.) Then proceed with the game. The second player must repeat the first person's item and name one of her own. For example, the first player might say, "I see a bird's nest." The second would reply, "I see a bird's nest and a daisy." The players continue recapping and adding items until one player forgets the sequence. The player who forgets is the loser. If a player names an item that the other player feels is not really within their sight, the second player may challenge the first player.

Extension

Memory skills can be improved through repetition and practice. Take every opportunity to help your child flex his "memory" muscles. If you're driving to the supermarket, ask your child which way to turn. If you're telephoning a friend, ask your child to memorize and use the phone number.

Try playing this memory game with your child. Tell him to observe your clothing, jewelry, and hair ornaments carefully. Have him leave the room or cover his eyes. Remove one piece of clothing, jewelry, or hair ornament. Have him name what you removed. If he succeeds, you leave the room and let him remove something. (If this sounds suspiciously like a teenage game of strip poker, do not despair. After each round, the removed items are put back on!)

The Art of the Picture Puzzle

½ hour

Kids love picture puzzles, especially ones they make themselves. Both the creation and the solution of the puzzle are a challenge, bringing mental and motor skills alike into play.

Supplies

Picture from a magazine or small art print
White craft glue
Cardboard
Pencil
Scissors
Brown wrapping paper (optional)

Directions

Select a suitable picture from a magazine or purchase an art print for your puzzle. Paste the picture onto a piece of cardboard that has been cut to size. Be careful not to crease the picture when pasting it down. (For a more professional, easy-to-handle puzzle, paste some brown wrapping paper, also cut to size, onto the back side of the cardboard.) Turn the picture over and have your child divide up the picture into puzzle-size pieces with his pencil. (Remember, the smaller the child, the bigger the pieces.) To cut out puzzle pieces, parental help may be needed.

Extension

Purchase a series of 9 x 12 art prints from your local art museum. Once your child has completed a series of three or more puzzles, take him to the museum and ask him to locate his puzzles on the museum walls.

Picture puzzles can also be used as birthday and greeting cards. Place the appropriate pictures and messages on the cardboard, then cut into puzzles, disassemble, and mail to friends and relatives for them to piece together.

Reading and

Language Arts

Do your children love to tell stories? Sing songs? Make up rhymes? Tell jokes? That's because they love to play with language. You can use their natural instinct for language to help foster their curiosity and imagination as well as to develop their language skills.

Language skills encompass reading, writing, speaking, and listening. Listening to you read or tell a story will inspire children to read, tell stories, and write on their own. When they hear you read, they become aware of how ideas and narratives develop. They discover the beauty of words and the rhythm of language. To help children take the step to reading on their own, point to words on a page. Follow sentences with your finger. Show pauses. Encourage them to turn the page for you. When it's time for writing, assure them that spelling is not scary. They don't always have to be accurate. Checking a writing exercise for spelling should be turned into a game instead of a test.

Power comes from knowledge. Books are full of it. Your children's world will continually grow and flourish with each new language adventure. Keep a shelf stacked with reading choices. If you want suggestions for material, obtain the brochures *Timeless Classics* and *Books for Children* from the U.S. Government Printing Office.

Movie Time

½ to ¾ hour

A picture tells a thousand words. An exciting way to inspire children to read is for them to create their own story with pictures. Sequencing pictures to build a story will keep the flow of imagination going.

Supplies

Long paper, e.g., rolled brown wrapping paper or a paper towel roll

Shoebox

Scissors

Two long cardboard tubes (from paper towels) or wooden dowels

Masking tape

Markers or crayons

Directions

Have your child draw scenes from an adventure story on long paper. You might suggest a topic if the child is hesitant, e.g., a space odyssey, a mystery in a castle, a journey in the wild west, a comedy in the park. Make holes on the sides of a shoebox big enough to insert tubes or dowels. Cut out a rectangular screen on the lid. Tape the front and back edge of the illustrated paper to each dowel. Roll the paper so that only the first scene of the story is in view. Tape the lid to the box. The child can now turn the dowels to move the scenes along as she tells the story.

Extension

The movie shoebox can be used for a variety of storytelling activities. Try it for a book or a poem you and your child have read. What about a journal that illustrates a special day in your child's life? Perhaps your child could draw scenes from a trip or vacation.

Half a Letter

½ hour

Symmetry is part of the natural order of things. Spider's webs, leaves, many geometrical shapes, butterflies, our faces—their designs are based on parts that are identical. You'll notice that your child will often automatically arrange a set of blocks symmetrically. Children have an intuitive understanding of the concept.

Supplies

> Marker
> Paper
> Small mirror (without a frame)

Directions

Help your child to print out the alphabet in capital letters on paper. Leave ample room between letters so that you can place a mirror on each one. Use the mirror to find the letters that have lines of symmetry. Place the mirror horizontally or vertically to discover the letters. For example:

B   M   O   X

Extension

Play a game with mystery half words. Help your child write short words with letters that are made up of lines of symmetry. The words can be written vertically or horizontally. In pencil, draw a line lightly to show where the letters of the word are divided into identical parts. For example:

M   O X

O

M

Erase half of the word's symmetry. Your child can now give a mirror and the half words to friends and ask them to discover the mystery word.

A Colorful Tale

¼ hour +

Supplies

None

Directions

Describe the following story scenario to your child: "In a magic kingdom, far far away, the royal family loved only one color." Explain that everything in the story has to have at least a bit of that color. You and your child can alternate sentences. If you choose the color yellow, for example, your story can begin this way: "In the Kingdom, it was <u>sunny</u>

everyday. There were <u>daffodils</u> everywhere. <u>Lemons</u> grew on the trees. Princess <u>Goldie</u> made <u>lemonade</u> from the fruit." (Note: the underlined words refer to things that are usually yellow.) Try this story with other colors.

Extension

Play a game with colors. See how many words you can list that have the name of a color in them, e.g., bluebird, pinky, greenhouse. Continue by choosing a color and then naming variations (shades) of that color, e.g., blue: navy, powder blue, turquoise.

Category Bingo

½ to 1 hour

This variation of bingo will build vocabulary as well as improve classification skills. Any number of people can play the game.

Supplies

Large blank index cards
Ruler
Marker
Pencil
Two or more players

Directions

Distribute index cards to each player. Have each player draw a bingo grid (5 squares across and 5 down with the center square colored in). The object of the game is to be first to fill as much of your card as possible in a given category. If very small children are involved, have group players where at least one player can spell. Call out a category and give the players at least 10 minutes to complete their card. Continue the game with a new bingo card for a different category. Here are some suggestions for categories: names of houses where humans or animals live (nest, hut), names of buildings (bank, store), animals (cat, rabbit), games (baseball, monopoly), toys (doll, marbles), names of things in a park (tree, bench), items of clothing (socks, hat).

Extension

Examine the cards and help your child read the bingo words. Can he/she use the words in a sentence? Talk about unknown words. Compare words on a card. If, for example, the category is human and animal homes, talk about how a nest is different from a cave and why.

Balloon Friend

½ hour

What are the qualities you look for in a good friend? Find out what your child's criteria are with the help of a new friend.

Supplies

Round balloon
Felt markers
Gummed label paper
Scissors

Decoration (e.g., streamers, wool, buttons)
Tape or string

Directions

Talk about what makes a good friend. Illustrate the characteristics by creating a friend, using a balloon. Blow up a round balloon and tie/tape it down to a chair or counter. Paint facial features and clothing patterns on the gummed paper with markers. Cut the shapes out and stick them onto the balloon. The child can tape other features to the balloon, such as streamers for hair. Talk about how the balloon person has the qualities of a good friend.

Create a story about the balloon person using "What if?" scenarios. Here are some examples: "What if the balloon could talk?" "What if the balloon floated up and took you away into the sky?" "What if the balloon could help you do anything you wanted?" "What if the balloon lived in a castle and you came for a visit?"

Extension

You might want to read Pheobe Gilman's *The Balloon Tree.* After talking about the book, you can make your own balloon tree with twigs, string, and balloons of varied shapes and colors.

ABC Sillies

¼ to ½ hour

This game cultivates practice in beginning phonics and creative expression. It's a fine activity for trips or sitting in a restaurant or waiting room.

Supplies

Pencil

Paper

Directions

Write the alphabet on a piece of paper. Using this paper as a reference, have your child make up sentences with words in alphabetical order. For example: "Alice better call Dr. Ed." The sentences can be very silly. Take turns with him and see who can make the longest sentence.

Extension

Your child can make a "goofy name chain" by writing a sentence using the letters of his name. Morgan: "Morgan ordered raw green animal noses!" Another variation is to try making sentences using words that all start with the same letter.

Giant Wordsearch

½ hour +

Wordsearch puzzles are among the first puzzles that children can solve. Beginning readers delight in deciphering
them, and making them is even more fun.

Supplies

Picture dictionary
Piece of scrap paper
Large piece of paper, at least 22" x 22"
Yardstick or long board
Pencil
Dark color marker

Directions

Help your child select fifteen or more words to include in
the wordsearch. If necessary, use the dictionary for inspiration. Have your child list the words on the scrap paper. Make
a grid on the large sheet to fill in with letters. Hold the yardstick for your child while she uses the pencil or marker to
make the grid lines. Be sure to leave space at the bottom of
the paper to list the wordsearch words. When the grid is
completed, have your child write in the wordsearch words
in pencil. Explain to her that they should be somewhat
evenly distributed throughout the grid. Interlocking words
are trickier to find and some should certainly be included.
When the words are all placed in the grid (and you're sure
there are no spelling errors), have your child go over them
with the dark marker. Next, she will fill in the rest of the grid
with random letters. When the whole puzzle is completed,
have her list the wordsearch words on the bottom of the

page. If possible, hang the wordsearch in a central location in your house. Your child will enjoy challenging adult and young visitors to find a word in the wordsearch.

Extension

Encourage your child to develop some thematic word-searches. For example, a Pets wordsearch would only include words that pertain to pets. A Family wordsearch would only contain names of people in the family. If you find that wordsearch fever has taken hold in your house, a pack of large-grid graph paper should make the project easier and more accessible.

Softer-Louder

½ hour

Do you remember playing "Hot and Cold" when you were a child? As you approached a hidden object, the other players would tell you if you were getting hotter or colder. You'll probably recognize "Softer-Louder" as a variation on that childhood favorite. In this version, your child has the fun of tracking down a hidden object while you reinforce the concept of soft and loud.

Supplies

Objects to hide

Directions

Show your child an object and explain that you are going to hide it somewhere in the room. Have him leave the room.

Call him back and have him start looking. As he walks toward the object, clap loudly. As he walks away from the object, clap softly. Increase or decrease intensity as appropriate. When your child has had a few turns as the hunter, switch roles. Leave the room while he hides something and let him guide you with hand claps.

Extension

This is also a wonderful game to play with a group of children. If your child's birthday party is coming up, you might consider this as a "Find the Party Favor" game. Hide the party favor bags (one by one) and let the clapping begin!

Face to Face

¼ to ½ hour

Good listening skills enable us to follow directions and process auditory information. Even the most intelligent child will have trouble in school if her listening skills are not up to par. This enjoyable activity serves the dual purpose of honing listening skills *and* providing a rollicking good time.

Supplies
None
Two players

Directions
The two players sit face to face. One player is "It." "It" names three body parts and touches them at the same time.

On the fourth turn, "It" names a body part but touches a different one. For example, if "It" says knee, he might touch his foot. The other player must listen to "It" and touch the parts "It" names. The challenge here is to do what "It" says, not what "It" does. If the player successfully follows "It's" verbal direction, the player gets to be "It." If not, "It" gets a turn to call the body parts again.

Extension

There are many things you can do to improve your child's listening skills. One good outdoor listening activity involves listening for nature sounds. Go outside with her and sit together quietly. How many sounds can she identify? Another good activity involves following directions. Give your child a simple sequence of two actions to perform—for example, "Touch your toes, and twirl around." If she has no trouble following two steps, add a third, a fourth, and so on. The object here is to increase your child's concentration. Make sure the tasks you name are fun; otherwise she may not be sufficiently motivated.

Alphabet Scavenger Hunt

¾ hour

Scavenger hunts have always been popular with children. Here's a way they can be educational, too. Don't be surprised if the hunt yields some unusual collections—children tend to be very imaginative scavengers!

Supplies

Piece of lined paper

Pencil

Directions

Write the letters of the alphabet on the paper, giving each letter its own line. Explain to your child that you want him to find one object to go with each letter of the alphabet. If you wish, you may permit him to hunt indoors and outdoors, restricting him to your backyard or immediate neighborhood. Once your child has found his 26 items, help him list each item next to its corresponding letter. For example, A for acorn, B for ball, C for cookie, etc. Some parents prefer to eliminate Q and Z from the alphabet, but resourceful children can usually come up with a quilt or zipper to fill the bill. If your child enjoys a more competitive task, use a kitchen timer to set a time limit on the hunt. You can also use this activity with groups of children working in teams of two.

Extension

You can vary this activity to make it more challenging. Ask your child to come up with more than one item per letter. Advanced readers, or children with older siblings who can help, can be asked to find items whose names end with select letters of the alphabet: harmonica for A, knob for B and so on. Stay away from c, f, h, i, j, o, q, u, v, x, z. Although some of these letters are not impossible, they're all very difficult.

Who Am I?

½ hour

Most kids know 101 nursery rhymes before they are four. Humpty Dumpty and Wee Willie Winkie are old pals and, with some help from you, are the subjects of a guessing game that stimulates young imaginations and starts the creative juices flowing.

Supplies

You and one or more children

Illustrated book of nursery rhymes, if needed, for consultation

Directions

Explain to the kids that "Who Am I?" is a guessing game that involves identifying nursery rhyme characters. You will start off by describing a character and see how many clues it takes before they can guess the character. For example, you might say, "I am an egg." Pause; if they don't guess, proceed with, "I sat on a wall." Then go on to "I fell off the wall," and so on. Take turns describing and guessing the characters.

Extension

"Who am I?" will send kids back to their nursery rhyme books to find new characters to stump you with. That's great; and in time, you may want to expand "Who Am I?" to include characters from fairy tales, thus opening up another rich lode for children to mine.

I Can Read

¼ hour +

As your child begins to acquire reading skills, it's important to encourage him in every way. This simple art activity will give him a way to express his pride in his most astonishing and exciting accomplishment to date—namely, reading!

Supplies

Strips of light colored paper about seven inches long and three inches wide

Stapler

Felt tip pens in various colors

Directions

Praise your child about his newfound reading ability. Have him write the name of each book he reads on a strip of paper, and then staple the strips together to start a chain. Challenge him to make a chain as long as the house, as big as the perimeter of the living room, or whatever length suits your house.

Facilitate him in every way by making sure to make weekly trips to the library. These days, with the widespread availability of inexpensive paperbacks, people often neglect the library. Do not fall into this trap. A library "habit" is like a passport to a successful future.

Extension

There are many other ways for your child to display his reading accomplishments. For example, you might help him make a "bookworm" whose body lengthens by another segment each time he completes a book. Another possibility is a thermometer-like gauge that your child can color as he goes from one to one hundred books.

When you make your weekly library trips, don't forget to use the services of the children's librarian. She can steer you and your child to age-appropriate and age-appealing books. Also, don't neglect the nonfiction shelves of the children's section. Youngsters have an almost insatiable thirst for knowledge, especially in the fields of particular interest. Many a five- and six-year-old will eagerly devour nonfiction.

Stepping Stone Game

¼ to ¾ hour

This is a versatile game format that can be modified over and over again to meet your child's ever-changing academic needs. Best of all, your child won't even realize he's playing an educational game!

Supplies

Sidewalk or concrete patio
Thick, washable colored chalk or
Large piece of tagboard
Marker pen

Directions

Draw large stepping stones in a continuous and somewhat irregular pattern on the tagboard or the concrete. Decide on a subject area you wish to review with your child. If, for example, you want him to review his consonant sounds, write a consonant on each stone. Explain to your child that the stones are like a bridge across a brook. Ask him to hop from stone to stone naming a word that begins with each letter. If he makes a mistake, or steps off a stone into the "brook," he needs to start again from the beginning. This game works well with one child but can also be played by two or more children competitively.

Extension

You can vary this game in an almost infinite number of ways. Here are just a few:

- ☉ Write a number on each stone and ask your child to tell you if each number is more or less than five.
- ☉ Write a word on each stone and ask your child to name a new word that rhymes with each word.
- ☉ Write a color name on each stone and ask your child to read the word and name a fruit or other food that color.
- ☉ Write a simple math problem on each stone and ask your child to solve each one.

Secret Sounds

¼ hour +

Most good thinkers are also good listeners. Listening is a skill that requires practice and refinement. Help your child develop this too-often neglected skill with the following activity.

Supplies

Tape recorder with microphone

Blank tape

Pencil and paper

Directions

Spend one day recording a variety of sounds in and around your home. Include an assortment of ordinary sounds such as a doorbell ringing, your dog barking, or popcorn popping, along with a selection of less common sounds such as bacon frying in a pan, someone brushing his teeth, and an electric fan whirring. Be sure to write down each sound in the order you record, as it is easy to forget. Record each sound for no more than thirty seconds. Play back the tape for your child. How many sounds can she correctly identify?

Extension

Your child can record her own sounds and play them back for you or a friend. It's also fun to record voices and see how many can be recognized. You don't have to restrict your choices to family voices; you can also include celebrity voices from records, radio, or TV.

Tee Shirt Phonics

½ to 1 hour

This homemade version of a popular tee shirt style gives your child practice in design, writing, and phonics.

Supplies

Clean, white or light-colored tee shirt

White drawing paper

Heavy black marker pen
Crayons (dark colors are best)
Iron

Directions

Explain to your child that you are going to make an alphabet tee shirt. Ask her to choose a letter from the alphabet that she wishes to feature on her shirt. Once she has chosen a letter, have her print it carefully with a heavy black marker on the drawing paper. Have her turn the paper over and trace over the letter with crayon on the reverse side. The heavy black line should show through. If it does not, print the letter for your child, but be sure to print it *backward*. This is the side she will be using to make her shirt. The letter will appear backward now but when it is printed it will reverse again. She can illustrate the (backward) letter with a picture of something that begins with the letter. For example, if she chooses C she may want to draw a cat or a car. (The drawing and letter must be small enough to fit on the front of the tee shirt.) Make sure she makes the letter rather thick and presses hard with her crayons (softly applied crayon will not transfer effectively).

Put the tee shirt on your ironing board. Place the drawing face down on the tee shirt. Use an iron that has been set for the right temperature for the tee shirt material. Transfer the drawing to the tee shirt by ironing over the drawing. Let the shirt cool, and voilà—an alphabet shirt!

Extension

You can use this method to make all kinds of different shirts. For example, is your child ecology-minded? Does your child want to launch a save-the-whales drive? If so, how about a tee shirt that features an appropriate slogan? Other possibilities are joke or riddle tee shirts, tongue twister shirts, word puzzle shirts, etc.

Highway Colors

1 hour +

Here's an easy-to-construct game that makes car trips seem shorter and enhances visual discrimination. You may recognize it as a variation on Bingo.

Supplies

Colored construction paper
Scissors
Glue
Empty egg cartons
Something to use as markers
   (coins, small squares of paper, beans, etc.)
Two or more players

Directions

Cut the colored paper into small circles or other shapes so that you can glue one into the bottom of each egg cup. Stick with the basics: red, yellow, blue, white, black, green, orange, brown. Vary the combination of colors so that each carton is different: some can have two reds, others two blues, etc. Each player gets an egg carton and markers. The driver or another adult watches the road and calls out, "I see a red car; I see a green sign; etc." The first player to fill her egg carton wins. The winner can be the caller on the next game.

Extension

For beginning readers, use color words on the bottom of each cup. You can also use letters of the alphabet instead of colors. If so, the driver or other adult calls out things such as "I see an *a*pple tree," and the child with an A on his carton places a marker in that cup.

Roadside Alphabet

½ hour +

This is another easy travel game that jogs beginning reading skills and visual acuity.

Supplies

None

Directions

Have your child look for billboards and road signs that begin with the letters of the alphabet in order. For example, first she must find a sign that advertises an "A" product such as "apple cider." Next, she needs to find a billboard that advertises something that begins with B such as "Bob's Cafe," and so on. It's fun for the whole family to join in, especially when you get to difficult letters like Q and Z.

Extension

Instruct your child to find objects in alphabetical order. "I see an alley. There's a bus, a car, and a dog." Here's another variation for older children: give out paper and pencil and have each child silently make a list of alphabetical objects. The first one to complete the list is the winner.

What's in a Name?

½ hour +

Here's an early reading game for kids who know their alphabets. Some children may actually learn to read a few words, while others will improve their letter recognition skills. Either way, your child will certainly benefit from the one-to-one quality time with you.

Supplies

Index cards or small note pad papers
Markers

Directions

Explain to your child that you are going to play a special game. Ask him to choose two or three items in his room or play area that he would like to label and use in the game. Prepare two index card labels for each item.

Pin or tape one label to each item. Examine each label with your child. Ask him to say the label name letters out loud. Go into another room. Hand your child a card and give him a direction such as, "Bring me this thing" or "Stand next to this thing." He must go back into his room and follow the direction. As he becomes more proficient at this game, you can increase the number of items and even reverse roles. If you like, you can add a reward for each correct response.

Decoder

½ hour +

Here's an activity that will expand your child's language skills and appeal to his sense of mystery.

Supplies

Paper and pencil

Directions

Explain to your child that codes are used for private communication. Point out that there are many different kinds of codes. Teach your child some of these codes and explain that he may use them with anyone to whom he chooses to give the "key."

Backward code: All words are simply written backward.
i evol uoy yrev hcum = i love you very much

Add-a-letter code: Choose a letter to place between every word.
iblovebyoubverybmuch = i love you very much

Letter substitutes: A = B, C = D, and so on
j mpwf zpv wfsz nvdi = i love you very much

Number substitutes: A = 1, B = 2, and so on
9, 12, 15, 22, 5, 25, 15, 21, 22, 5, 18, 25, 13, 21, 3, 8

Extension

Encourage your child to make up her own code using any combination of letters, numbers, or symbols. It might be fun to set up a message box where family members can leave code notes for each other.

Word for a Day

¼ hour +

This simple activity is based on the Language Experience Approach to reading. Basically, the underlying philosophy is that children learn best when the words they are reading are meaningful to them. Word for a Day will help develop your child's reading vocabulary and reinforce his alphabetization skills.

Supplies

File box
Index cards
Alphabetical dividers for the file box
Assorted markers
Stickers

Directions

Explain to your child that you are going to start something new that you and he can do together every day. Show him the box and tell him that this will be his word box. Each day he may pick a word that he would like to add to his box and you will write it for him on an index card.

Let him choose a word to start the collection. If he's stumped for an idea, tell him what you and he will be doing together that day. Is a friend coming to visit? Perhaps he'd like to use the word "zoo." Print the word on the card for him and show him how to file it alphabetically. Encourage him to use the stickers and markers to decorate his word box.

Be sure to review old words every day. Add new words every other day unless you feel your child can handle a new one every day. In a few weeks your child may well have a small, personalized reading vocabulary. A note of caution: don't be alarmed if your child does not remember all the words. The important thing here is to give your child a positive and pleasurable experience with language. If you put pressure on him to perform, you are defeating the purpose of this activity.

Extension

You may also want to use the word collection to encourage your child to improve his oral expression. Have him take two or three cards from the file and use them in sentences or make them part of an original story. If your child needs to practice his printing, consider having him print each word under yours.

The Thanksgiving Tradition Touch

½ hour

Sometimes we all need to be reminded that holidays are not just excuses for gluttony and family gatherings. Use this Thanksgiving activity a day or two before hosting or going to a Thanksgiving celebration. It's great for stimulating creative writing and it's also a wonderful character builder. The whole family can benefit from this opportunity to express appreciation for others.

Supplies

Construction paper
Assorted felt tip markers
Envelopes

Directions

Explain to your child that the first Thanksgiving was essentially a feast to thank God and the North American Indians for helping the pilgrims survive a harsh winter in their new homeland. Ask if he's ever felt thankful for anything. How about his birthday present? Or the time his big sister shared her popcorn with him? Help him arrive at several examples of times when he's felt thankful.

Show your child the construction paper. Would he like to make cards to thank people for some of the nice things they have done for him? Help him choose a person and discuss what he'd like to thank that person for. Did Grandpa help him learn to use a fishing rod? Did Grandma knit him a sweater? Does his aunt take care of him after nursery school? There are bound to be many reasons for your child to express his thanks.

Together you can draw a Thanksgiving motif on the outside of his card and compose a message that begins, "I am thankful for you, Grandpa, because you . . ." Encourage your child to make as many of these cards as he wishes.

Extension

Print the names of everyone who is coming to your Thanksgiving celebration. Put the names in a hat. Have each guest draw a name from the hat. After dinner, but before dessert, have each person say something nice about the person whose name he drew. This is a wonderful self-esteem builder for young and old alike. (If you prefer, you can have each person thank someone for something they did, but that's a bit harder to pull off unless everyone in the room is well acquainted.)

Invisible Ink

¼ to ½ hour

Here's an irresistible way to motivate your child to use her writing skills. Secret messages to friends, thank-you notes to relatives, will all flow from her pen when she's learned the secret of invisible ink.

Supplies

> Lemon
> Bowl
> Straight tip pen
> Paper
> Iron

Directions

Have your child squeeze lemon juice into a bowl. Direct her to dip a clean straight pen into the lemon juice and then write a message on a piece of paper. The message will show up when the paper is pressed with a very hot iron. (Naturally, this part can only be done by an adult.) Magic? No, the acid in the lemon juice makes the invisible ink.

Extension

A related project would be to introduce your child to berry ink. Simply crush blackberries, blueberries, or strawberries in a bowl, add water, and mash through a strainer. The berry juice is your ink—and one of the earliest kinds of writing ink!

Talk to your child about the origin of ink. Ink was invented by ancient Egyptians and Chinese. No one knows exactly when it was invented but there is evidence of manuscripts written in ink as far back as 2000 B.C.

Math

Parents often think that doing math with children is more difficult and less fun than doing reading or art. But math can be just as exciting. Unlike the way we as adults learned math, children learn it in terms of creative problem-solving where there is more than one way to arrive at an answer. Math is more than the calculation of numbers. It's making choices, examining relationships, using reasoning, and exploring possibilities.

Look around you. Math is everywhere. The difficulty with not seeing it comes from our own learning. What we see doesn't look anything like the math we did in school. But every time you buy groceries, plant a flower bed, play the piano, or even plan your day—you're using math. You can use such everyday tasks to involve your children in math. Use a pie to show fractions. Check a schedule to teach time. Take advantage of a trip to find numbers. Do lots of mental math with ordinary things, for example, "If you eat two of these five cookies, how many did you leave for me?" Estimating too is a good mental math activity. Try guessing the number of pickles in a jar or tacks in a box.

A crucial ingredient in any activity you do with your children is to help them develop a positive attitude toward math. Turn a wrong answer into an exploration of how and why your child arrived at an answer. Sometimes a child sees the problem differently from you. For example, "2 + __ = 5" could have been interpreted as "2 + 5." The response of "7," then, is a reasonable answer. Asking your child to explain the response will show you how to help find the right or "more reasonable" answer.

Tic-Tac-Toe-Twelve

¼ to ½ hour

This game is similar to Tic-Tac-Toe, i.e., players take turns trying to complete a row across, down, or diagonally. In this math version, players use numbers instead of X or O.

Supplies

Pad of paper
Two different-colored markers, e.g., red and green
One black marker
Two players

Directions

Draw tic-tac-toe grids with a black marker on as many pieces of paper as will take to play the game in the time suggested. The grid consists of three squares down and three across. Give two differently-colored markers to each player. The goal of the game is for each player to mark a spot with his/her personal marker on the grid with a number from one to nine. A number may be used more than once in the game. The winner is the player whose numbers add up to twelve in any row—vertically, diagonally, or horizontally.

Extension

To make the game a little more challenging, restrict the use of any or all numbers to once in each game.

Plus & Minus Cards

½ to ¾ hour

A deck of cards provides a lot of opportunities for all kinds of mathematical skills. This game focuses on adding and subtracting.

Supplies

Deck of cards
Note paper
Pencil
Two or more players

Directions

Sort through the deck to keep only cards with values from two to nine, for a total of thirty-two cards. Each player gets a chance at being the dealer, in clockwise order. The dealer shuffles the cards and deals out two cards to each player, including him or herself. No one can look at the cards until the dealer calls out a "goal" number between five and ten. Players then take turns drawing from the deck and discarding one card per turn in order to make their cards add up to the dealer's "goal" number. The first player whose cards match the dealer's "goal" number wins the round and gets a point. Any player can make calculations on paper during the game, if necessary. Continue the game with each dealer calling a different "goal" number. You can set the limit of rounds at the beginning of the game, e.g., the first player to get ten points wins the game. Keep score for each player on paper.

Extension

To vary the game, increase the "goal numbers," for example,

from five to fifteen. You can also make the game more difficult by playing the game with three cards and calling "goal" numbers between ten and twenty or twenty-five. In each variation, make sure the spread between "goal numbers" is at least five and no more than fifteen.

Mystery Number

¼ hour

Math patterns will intrigue your child, while sharpening his/her observation skills. You can even extend math patterns to geometry which will help develop spatial perceptions. This activity calls for one die. Somewhere in the house you will have a board game that requires dice for playing.

Supplies
> One die
> Paper
> Pencil

Directions
Set up a chart on paper in this way:
> Roll   1 2 3 4 5 6 7 8 9 10
> Dots on top
> Dots on bottom

Ask your child to roll the die. After each roll, write on the chart the number of dots on top of the die. Then lift the die carefully and record the number of dots on the bottom. Do the same for ten rolls of the die.

Have your child examine the pairs of numbers for each roll. How is each pair the same as all the other pairs. Hint: add each pair up to discover the mystery number.

Extension

Find a small empty box that is a cube or construct one using stiff paper and tape. Have your child create a die by painting dots on its surface. Turn the activity into a puzzle. After painting dots on one side of the die, have the child guess the number of dots on the opposite surface before painting it (they already know that the opposite sides always add up to 7). After the die is complete, you may want to unfold the cube to show how it looks when it is flat. Talk about how flat surfaces, when they are shaped to enclose volume, become 3-D shapes. Give examples of flat shapes compared with 3-D shapes, for example, a triangle and a pyramid. Unfold and reassemble other small containers, for example, a cereal box.

Multiplying Mirrors

½ hour +

Does your child have a piggy bank? Here's a game that will demonstrate how to increase his/her savings.

Supplies

    Two small mirrors
    Masking tape
    Penny
    Nickel

Dime
Quarter
Note paper
Pencil

Directions

Tape the two mirrors together. They should be loose enough so that you can vary the angle at which they intersect. Stand the mirrors up on a table. Place a penny between them and watch them multiply. Vary the angle to see how many pennies you can see. Do the same with a nickel, dime, and quarter. What is the most money you can make with each coin? Write your calculations and totals on paper, if necessary.

Extension

You can use small objects to practice multiplication. Try pencils, buttons, pasta, etc. What about using three mirrors. Can you make your savings or objects grow even more?

License Plates

Time depends on your travel time

You probably spend a lot of time in transit with your child. Use your travel time to help your child with math. There are numbers everywhere, on buildings, on vehicles, on road signs and billboards.

Supplies

Paper
Pencil

Directions

Before setting out on your journey, show your child your car's license plate. Explain its purpose. Record it on a piece of paper. En route to your destination, ask your child to copy down the numbers (not letters) of license plates. See if your child can read them out as a number. Then have him/her compare your license number with the recorded plates. Is your number less than, greater than, or equal to the numbers on the list? You may want to have your child add up the numbers for each plate recorded, for example, if the license plate read 243•621, then the sum total would be 18.

Extension

You may want to ask your child to stay on the lookout for phone numbers on the sides of taxis and trucks or numbers on buildings during the trip home. The child can record the numbers on a piece of paper. At home, you can conduct a review and compare numbers in the same way as you did with the license plates.

Clock Game

¼ to ½ hour

This geometry game is played on any polygon, i.e., any shape with three or more sides. It has been modified to teach your child how to read a clock. The original version of the game is provided in the extension activity.

Supplies

Large piece of stiff cardboard

Ruler
Markers
Object from which to trace circles, e.g., jar lid, quarter
Twelve pennies
Two players

Directions

Draw a shape with 12 equal sides (dodecagon) using a ruler and markers. At each vertex (where two sides meet), trace a circle. Write numbers representing the hours of a clock in each circle. Before the game, discuss how to tell time by the hour with your child, for example, one o'clock. To play the clock game, use pennies for markers. One player calls an hour and the other player places his/her marker on the appropriate number OR the two adjacent numbers. For example, if player A calls 3 o'clock, player B can place a penny on 3 o'clock or a penny each on 4 o'clock and 5 o'clock. The player to place the last marker wins. After some time, expand your child's knowledge by tracing circles where the 5-minute mark would be on a clock and playing the game by calling "five after/before" the hour. You can play the game to show how to read ten minutes past/before the hour, half past the hour, etc. Have you discovered the sure-win strategy? When it's your turn, make sure your play mirrors that of your opponent.

Extension

Play the original game with any polygon, e.g., triangle, square, hexagon, etc. You do not have to trace circles or write any numbers like in the clock game. Place pennies on all the vertices of the shape. Each player in turn picks up one marker or two adjacent markers. The player to pick up the last marker wins. Does the sure-win strategy apply for all shapes? The clock game used a shape with an equal number of sides. What was your strategy for polygons with an odd number of sides?

Guesstimating

¼ to ½ hour

You may be surprised to find that guessing how many jelly beans are in a jar is a serious math task. It takes practice to master estimation, a basic component of problem solving. Have fun with this!

Supplies

Cheerios or any other similar dry cereal
Cereal bowl
Two or more players

Directions

Fill the bowl with cereal. How many pieces of cereal are in the bowl? Have everyone write down a guess. Count the pieces. The one who comes closest can gobble up the cereal.

Here's a simple way to help your child avoid making wild guesses in this game. Give him a handful of cereal which he can count. Have him base his estimate on how many handfuls of cereal he thinks will fit into the bowl. (If necessary, help him add up the numbers. Remember, this activity is meant to teach estimating, not computation skills.)

Extension

Since estimating does require practice, try the same activity using different items. Here are some suggestions: How many grains in a quarter cup of rice? How many feet in a ball of yarn? How many paper clips in a bag? How many tablespoons of water in a glass?

Knock 'Em Down, Add 'Em Up

½ hour

This is a homemade version of a familiar carnival game. Unlike the carnival game, this one is easy to win and also reinforces addition or, for the mathematically precocious, multiplication skills.

Supplies

> Five to ten empty toilet paper rolls, tin cans, or cylindrical oatmeal containers
> Felt marking pen
> Paper and tape
> Wooden board propped up across chairs
> Tennis or similarly sized rubber balls

Directions

Write a number between 1 and 10 on the bottom of each oatmeal container. Each container should have a different number. If you're using tin cans, write the numbers on little squares of paper and tape the numbers to the bottoms of the cans. If you're using toilet paper rolls, write the numbers on the inside. Line up the containers, toilet paper rolls, or cans on the board. Space them approximately three inches apart. Have your child throw the ball and try to knock down a can.

When she has knocked down two, have her add up the numbers. Choose an arbitrary "winning" score to end the game. If you prefer, this can be a competitive game between you and your child or a group of children.

Extension

This game can be played several different ways. Numbers can be multiplied, subtracted, or even divided. Cans can also be lined up on the ground in a bowling pin configuration.

The Long and Short of It

1/2 hour +

This activity is a good introduction to measurement skills. Instead of using rulers, children use paper clip chains to measure common household objects and people.

Supplies

Full box of paper clips
   (large size ones are easiest for youngsters to handle)
Paper and pencil
Common household objects

Directions

Show your child how to clip the paper clips together to make a chain. Have him start by making a chain as tall as himself. Can he guess how many paper clips long his chain will be? Have him write down his guess. When the chain is complete, he can compare the actual number of clips against his guess. Now, can he guess how many clips tall you are?

Have him write down his guess and expand his chain.

Next, have your child find some objects in the house that are five clips tall (or long), ten clips tall, etc. How many objects can he find that are almost the same height or length as he is? The same size or length as you are?

Extension

Have your child measure and compare the dimensions of his room with your room. Which is larger? Ask him to determine which room in your house is smallest and which is largest. In both instances, let him make a prediction before he actually uses his paper clip chain to measure. (He will probably need your help "marking" and keeping track of each length of chain as he moves around the rooms.)

Show your child a tape measure and compare his paper clip chain to it. Point out the advantage of a flexible "ruler"—it can measure around things like waists and conform to curves.

Small, Medium, Large

¼ to ½ hour

Young children need lots of experience observing size relationships and making comparisons. This activity may seem extremely simple to us as adults, but for youngsters it can be quite a challenge.

Supplies

Plastic storage containers of various sizes with lids, or glass jars with lids

Directions

Set the containers out on a table and ask your child to find the matching lids. If she has trouble with this activity, help her develop a system for eliminating the possibilities one by one. If you are using glass jars, set them out on a rug or other padded area and supervise her closely to avoid accidents.

Extension

Assemble a small collection of nuts and bolts in different sizes. Show your child how they screw together and challenge her to find the matching nuts and bolts.

You can also use nesting measuring cups to reinforce this activity. Your child will enjoy stacking them in "size places."

The next time you go to the grocery store with your child, you may want to point out the different size packages. For example, laundry detergents come in various quantities. Which boxes are largest, which are smallest?

Odd or Even?

½ hour

In this activity, you may use raisins to teach your child the difference between odd and even numbers. If your child is not a raisin fan, consider using something a bit more tailored to her tastes, such as peanuts or cherries—anything small and edible will do.

Supplies

Box of raisins

Paper and pencil

Directions

On a piece of paper, write the numbers 1 to 10 and show them to your child. Explain that some of these numbers are called *odd* numbers and some of them are called *even* numbers. The object of this game is for her to guess which numbers are odd and which are even. To help her do this, tell her the key difference between even and odd numbers: Even numbers can be split into two equal groups but odd numbers cannot.

Demonstrate this principle by placing a group of six raisins on the table. Ask your child the following: "If you and I were sharing these raisins, how could we divide them up so that you and I would have the same number of raisins?" If necessary, help her through this process by saying, "One for me and one for you," and so on. When the raisins are properly divided, ask, "Were we able to divide six raisins into two equal groups—or two groups of the same size?" Point out that you have just demonstrated that six is an even number. Repeat the fact that even numbers can be divided into two equal groups. Allow your child to eat her share of the six raisins.

Have your child go through this process for each number on the list. After she has attempted to split each number into two groups, ask her if the number was odd or even, then have her put an O next to the number if it's odd, and E next to it if it's even. Keep reinforcing the definition of odd and even as you go along. By the time she's gone through the list, your child should have a pretty good grasp of this important mathematical concept.

Extension

Here's a traditional game for two players that will give your child additional practice in identifying odd and even numbers. One player is the odd team and the other is the even team. They face each other and say, "One, two, three, shoot." On the word "shoot," they each extend one, two, or three fingers from one hand. If the sum total of fingers is odd, the odd team player gets a point, if the sum total is even, the even team player gets a point. Ten points wins.

Snake Eye

½ to ¾ hour

This simple activity will give your child lots of counting practice and develop his sense of one-to-one correspondence. The game ends with a small popcorn feast, so plan to play Snake Eye at snack time.

Supplies

Pencil
One pair of ordinary dice
Two wooden blocks (plain cubes from a child's block set are perfect)
Felt markers
Popcorn (or other healthy snack in small pieces)
Two players

Directions

Show your child the ordinary dice and have him examine the dots on each face. Explain that you want to make a larger set of dice with dots that are easier to see and count. He can use the pencil to make the appropriate number of dots on each face of the wooden blocks. Have him count the dots as he marks them. When all the dots are correctly marked, he can go over the dots with the felt markers. Give the ink time to dry so that the dots will not smudge when you start the game.

Players take turns throwing one die at a time and counting the number of dots on the upward face. Two dots earn two pieces of popcorn and so on. If you throw a one (snake eye), you lose one piece.

Preset a time limit for the game and, when the time is up, count the number of pieces you each have to determine who won. Winners and losers alike eat their popcorn pieces as a tasty conclusion to this basic math game.

Extension

If your child is ready for a challenge, play this game with two dice. With two dice, snake eyes would forfeit two pieces. Once he is proficient at counting the dots on two dice at a time by pointing at each dot and counting 1, 2, 3, 4, etc., have him start adding up the sum of the dots on each die (such as one plus three make four).

Another way to extend this activity involves a research trip to the library. Ask your child if he can guess why the dice are called snake eyes when he throws a double one. Your local librarian can assist you both in finding out the origin of this colorful expression, and perhaps pique your child's interest in etymology.

A-Marketing We Will Go

1 hour +

Here's a way to combine imaginative role playing with math fundamentals. Your child will enjoy playing grocer while she begins to understand the value of the penny, nickel, and dime.

Supplies

Pennies, nickels, and dimes
Canned foods
Boxed foods
Adhesive labels
Markers
Construction paper
Tape

Directions

Show your child a penny, a nickel, and a dime. Explain that the penny stands for one cent, the nickel for five, and the dime for ten. Ask which is worth the most money. Help your child realize that the dime is worth the most, the nickel less, and the penny the least.

Explain to your child that you are going to let her set up her own store to shop in with her friends and dolls. Provide your child with a variety of pantry items and ask her to decide which ones should cost a penny, a nickel, and a dime. Show her how to write 1¢, 5¢, and 10¢ on the price labels. Have her prepare labels and affix them to the food items. Have her sort her items either according to price or according to food type (nonfood items like paper towels can be used too) and place them into groups on a table. If she wishes, she may make a "Sally's Market" sign to tape to the table.

Take turns with your child being the shopper and the shopkeeper. Be sure to use the coins to buy items. If your child is the shopkeeper, require her to tell you how much each item costs and whether you need to give her a penny, a nickel, or a dime. If your child is the shopper, let her decide which coins she needs to use to pay.

Extension

When your child is ready, begin to teach her about equivalent values. Have a coin exchange where she gets five pennies for a nickel, two nickels for a dime, and so on. Be sure to emphasize that having more coins does not necessarily mean having more money.

Shape Builders

½ to ¾ hour

Learning to identify geometric shapes is easier when children have first-hand experience making and manipulating them. This simple activity will reinforce shape recognition and provide hours of creative fun.

Supplies

One or more bags of dried peas
One or more boxes of toothpicks

Directions

Soak the peas overnight. In the morning, they should be softened and easy to poke with a toothpick. Show your child how to make simple shapes with the peas and toothpicks. (The peas act as joints and hold the toothpicks in place.)

Challenge your child to make a square using four toothpicks, eight toothpicks, etc. Ask her to make a triangle using three toothpicks, six toothpicks, and so on. Once you've worked with the basic shapes, introduce a few sophisticated shapes. For example, make a pentagon and ask your child to reproduce it.

Extension

Use your pea and toothpick building set to create all kinds of buildings, molecules, and designs. Colored toothpicks would be a nice alternative to plain ones, adding another dimension to the activity.

Addition Magician

½ to 1 hour

In this fun-to-do activity kids make a "magic hat" to play a simple addition game. Addition Magician is a painless way to practice basic addition skills up to the total of 18.

Supplies

Two paper cups
Black construction paper
Scissors
Tape
Tagboard or other stiff paper
Markers
Four dried beans or peas
Ruler
Two or more players

Directions

The paper cups will become the "magic hats" for this game. Cut a piece of black construction paper to wrap around and cover each paper cup. Be sure to cut discs to cover the bottoms of the cups. Also, cut rims that can be taped on as hat brims. (See diagram for examples.) Have players tape on the black paper to prepare their cups.

From the tagboard, cut a 9" x 9" gameboard for each player. Using a ruler, make a 3 box by 3 box grid on each gameboard. Have your child write a number between 1 and 9 in each box. Be sure that he includes all nine numbers on his board (no repeats allowed). Give each player two beans.

Have players place their beans in their magic hats. Players take turns tossing their beans on their gameboards. As a player tosses his beans, he says, "Alakazam . . . addition magician!" He then adds together the two numbers he lands on. Players receive one point for each correct sum. The player with the most points wins.

Extension

Like most simple grid games, Addition Magician can be adapted for many different kinds of skill practice. For example, numbers can also be subtracted or multiplied. Another variation is to write simple words in the grid and have players read the words they land on and use them in sentences.

Contortion

½ hour

This is the kind of game kids want to play over and over again. As you'll see, it's versatile enough to reinforce any number of skills including math, vocabulary, and color recognition. In this version, youngsters practice reading their number words.

Supplies

Piece of plain, light color fabric approximately 4' x 4'
Felt markers
Large index cards
Tape or bricks
Two or more players

Directions

Draw ten circles on the fabric in a hopscotch-like pattern of three circles, two circles, three circles, and two circles. In each circle write a number word. Write each number word on an index card. Place the index cards face down in a pile. Spread the fabric out on the floor or lawn. (Anchor the fabric with tape or, if outdoors, bricks.)

Players take turns drawing index cards. If a player draws a two, he places one hand or one foot on the "two" circle. On his next turn, he places another hand or foot on his next number card choice. The game continues until one player is so contorted that he loses his balance and cannot stay on the "board."

Extension

Almost anything can be written in the circles on the fabric. If you wish, you can write numerals and, on the index cards, simple math problems. If a child chooses the 2 + 2 card, he has to place his hand or foot on a 4, and so on. Another option is to draw geometric shapes on the circles and write their names on the index cards.

Still another approach is to devise a matching game that involves words and pictures. For example, the fabric circles would have concept words on them like tall, short, fat, thin. The corresponding index cards would contain simple line drawings or magazine pictures depicting each concept.

Survey

½ hour +

Graphing is an important math skill that children can grasp at a very young age. Bar graphs are particularly appropriate for four- to six-year-olds and can easily be adapted to cover many different areas of interest.

Supplies

Large piece of white paper
Felt markers
Magazines for cutting
Scissors
Glue or tape

Directions

Tell your child that you would like to find out if more people like vanilla or chocolate ice cream (any two foods will do, but these are good initial choices). Explain that for the next few days you would like her to ask everyone who comes into the house, everyone in the family, and everyone who phones which of the two flavors they prefer. Show her how to use a graph to keep track of the results. Draw two bar graph grids on the white paper. Have your child thumb through the magazines to find a picture of vanilla ice cream and one of chocolate ice cream. She can cut out the pictures and glue or tape one picture above each grid. (If no pictures are available, help her draw pictures of chocolate and vanilla ice cream cones.)

Start the graph by asking your child which flavor she prefers. Show her how to indicate her preference by coloring in a block on the grid. Next, tell her your preference and have her color in the appropriate space. For the next few days, have your child survey more people. When she's done, help her compare the results.

Extension

Once your inquisitive statistician experiences the lure of statistics, she can use the basic bar graph grid to survey many different things—for example, favorite television programs, activities, and favorite books.

Shape Toss

1 hour +

Shape Toss provides practice in identifying geometric shapes and also helps your child improve his gross motor skills. This is a great activity for a rainy day since it's physical but not rowdy.

Supplies

Fabric

Templates for making a circle, a square, a rectangle, and a triangle (make these from cardboard with a compass and ruler)

Felt markers

Scissors

Needle and thread

Dried beans or peas

Large cardboard box

Two or more players

Directions

Have your child trace two triangles, two circles, two squares, and two rectangles onto the fabric. She will use these shapes to make bean bags, so make sure your templates are large enough to make good size bags. Have your child cut out the shapes. Sew them on a sewing machine or with a needle and thread. Leave space to stuff them with the beans and close up when stuffed.

Invert the carton so that the bottom is facing up, like a tabletop. Draw a circle, a square, a triangle, and a rectangle on the carton. Make sure these shapes are larger than the bean bags by an inch or two all around. Cut out the shapes so that the box has four openings. Label each opening appropriately.

Players take turns tossing the bean bags. As each player takes his turn he states what he is throwing and how many sides it has. (In the case of the circle, he simply states that it's round.) If the bag goes in the proper hole, the player scores a point and gets another turn. If the bag goes through the wrong hole, the player gets to throw again. If the player misses altogether, he forfeits his turn and the next player goes. The game is over when a set number of points is reached or the players decide to quit.

Extension

If your child is ready to learn more shapes, make a more elaborate Shape Toss set. Add a pentagon, hexagon, oval, and diamond.

Fivepenny Morris

½ to 1 hour

This logic and strategy game is so old that it's even mentioned in Shakespeare's *Midsummer Night's Dream*. Today, it is still played in many different European nations including France, where it is called "Merilles," and Germany, where it is called "Muhl." Although its English name is traditional, I have not been able to discover its origin.

Supplies

Piece of cardboard or posterboard about 12 to 16 inches square
Two small sheets of colored posterboard or cardboard
 (two different colors)
Two players

Directions

Use the square piece of posterboard to make a gameboard. Draw three concentric squares and intermediary lines as shown in the diagram. Draw circles to indicate game spaces. Use the colored pieces of posterboard to make nine ½" diameter circular markers for each player. To play, players take turns putting their markers on the game spaces. The object is to place three markers in a row (diagonal placement does not count). When a player gets three in a row, she may remove one of her opponent's pieces. She may not remove a piece that was already settled in a three-in-a-row position. After all the pieces are placed, play continues with players moving their markers along the lines, one space at a time. The game is over when one player has only two markers left.

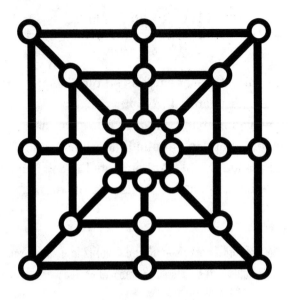

Extension

This game can be played outdoors on a chalk-drawn game-board. Players use different colors of chalk and erase "captured" opponents' markers.

Gelatin Giggles

½ to ¾ hour

Cooking is a great activity to share with your children and this cooking project is delightfully seasoned with a gaggle of giggles. It gives children practice in following directions and counting. One word of caution, if you're squeamish about messy faces, pass this one by!

Supplies

Box of flavored gelatin mix

Heavy cream for whipping (or, if you're in a hurry, use canned whipped cream)

Eggbeater

Two or more children (the more the merrier)

Blindfold(s)

Directions

Prepare the gelatin according to the directions on the package. If you don't want to wait for the gelatin to set, follow the speed set instructions. Next, have the children take turns whipping the cream. Tell them they may each turn the beater twenty times before passing it on to the next child. Have each child count her beater turns aloud. This may take some time but it's an excellent way to reinforce counting skills. If the beating becomes tedious, you may want to use an electric beater to finish off the job quickly. When the gelatin is set, divide it into individual serving bowls and put a dollop of whipped cream on each serving. Now the real fun begins. Assign each child a partner and blindfold one partner on each team. The object of the game is for the blindfolded partner to feed the other partner with a spoon. The first team to finish its serving wins the game. As you can well imagine, this game is a slippery, silly mess. Happy eating!

Extension

This activity can be enriched by varying the counting tasks. If your child can count beyond 20, by all means increase the number of turns per child. Another option is to ask your child to count his turns by fives, tens, or hundreds. For advanced mathematicians, keeping track of the total number of beats would be an exciting challenge.

Cranberries and Popcorn—
A Chain for Your Christmas Tree

½ to 2 hours

Cranberry and popcorn chains are traditional Christmas tree decorations. These chains are as simple as they are handsome. Children enjoy making chains that are one, two, or three times their own size. Another benefit: chainmaking is a perfect opportunity to teach your child about patterns—an important math basic.

Supplies

Index card
Two felt-tipped markers, one red, one yellow
Popcorn
Cranberries
Needle
Heavy thread
Glitter (optional)

Directions

On an index card, create a repeat pattern of circles. For example, draw a yellow circle, a red circle, a yellow circle, a red circle, and so on. Show your child the pattern and explain that it is called a "repeat pattern" because it repeats itself. Now draw a more complicated repeat pattern such as two yellows, a red, two yellows, a red, and so on. Help your child understand how this pattern works.

Once you're confident that your child understands the concept of the repeat pattern, have her create her own. Explain that she will be threading her popcorn and cranberry chain using this pattern. (Yellow circles stand for popcorn and red stand for cranberries.) Thread the needle for your child, knot the end, and let her "chain" away. If she gets tired of her pattern, encourage her to create a new one. (Your child may need help piercing an occasional cranberry, and you will lose some popcorn to hungry mouths or breakage, but don't give up. Most kids can manage the chain with some practice.) For a modern touch, place chains on newspaper and have kids spray with glitter.

Extension

Make this a family night. Get one of the older children to begin reading Dickens's *A Christmas Carol* or Moore's *The Night Before Christmas*. Share with your kids some of the things your family did to celebrate the holiday season.

A Weighty Question

½ hour +

If you have a bathroom scale you already know that young children love to weigh themselves. You can put this fascination to good use by making the bathroom scale part of a math measurement game designed to help your child make comparisons and predictions.

Supplies

    Bathroom scale
    Various household objects

Directions

If necessary, introduce your child to the scale. Point out that the numbers register how many pounds something weighs. The heavier an object, the more pounds it weighs. Ask your child to predict who will weigh more—he or you? After asking your child how he can test his prediction, take turns on the scale to test his hypothesis.

Now show your child two household objects and ask him to predict which object will be heavier. (Be sure the two objects are at least a pound apart in weight so that you do not have to compare fractions of a pound.) Give him the go-ahead on testing.

Extension

As your child weighs and compares objects, have him record their weights in nearest whole numbers. Later, when another teenage or adult family member returns home, have your child display his object collection and ask the person to guess which item is heaviest, lightest, etc. Your child will enjoy using his results to test an older and so-called "wiser" challenger.

Television Tally

½ hour +

This activity will turn Saturday morning cartoon viewing into a valuable learning experience. It's a great introduction to graphing and will also make your child aware of the ways in which the media attempt to influence our buying behavior.

Supplies
TV
Large white paper
Ruler
Assorted felt tip markers

Directions

Ask your child if she knows why television shows have commercials. Explain that advertisers pay for the time and that this money indirectly goes toward the cost of television production. Ask if she's ever noticed how many commercials her favorite television shows have and if she would like to do a comparison.

Help your child prepare a grid on the paper for a bar graph and show her how to use the graph to chart the number of commercials on each of her favorite TV shows. Have her label each bar with either the name of the show or a picture that symbolizes the show. As she watches her favorite show(s), sit with her and help her begin to color in her graph.

While she does so, discuss the content of the commercials with her. Does she really think that the latest doll is "just like a real baby"? Does she believe that the latest cereal will actually make her stronger or happier? Even a four-year-old is not too young to learn about truth in advertising. Children need to understand that not everything they hear on television should be taken at face value.

Extension

Help your child use a stopwatch or watch with an easy-to-read second hand to determine how much time is devoted to commercials on each of her favorite shows. Graph these results and compare them to some adult shows such as the evening news or a sitcom. Are there certain types of shows that devote more time to programming than others? What might these results mean?

Have you ever noticed that commercials are louder than the regular shows? Have your child close her eyes to test this out. Ask her if she can guess why the commercials are louder.

Christmas or Chanukah Calendar

2 to 3 hours

Use this activity to help your child learn to read and use a calendar. As a plus, your child's Christmas or Chanukah Calendar will make a terrific gift for a grandparent or other adult relative.

Supplies
Wall or desk calendar (preferably with illustrations)
White construction paper (or other heavy paper)
Ruler
Pencil
Colored markers or crayons
Paper fasteners or stapler

Directions
Show your child the calendar, mentioning that there is a page for each month of the year. Flip through the pages and show her how special holidays are illustrated or otherwise graphically noted. Point out how the calendar is laid out in

terms of days of the week and dates. Explain to your child that you are going to help her make a calendar that she can use either for herself or as a gift for someone. Cut twelve pieces of white paper approximately 16" x 8 ½". Holding the paper vertically, draw a line across the upper third of each page. Use the ruler to draw a grid on the lower two-thirds of the paper. Help your child write the days of the week along the top of the grid. From this point on have your child work on one page at a time. Have her label the first page "January" and help her fill in the dates beginning with one and ending with thirty-one. Make sure she starts on the correct day of the week. Remind your child that some months are longer than others and review the number of days in each month.

In the upper third of the paper have your child draw a picture for January. She may want to draw a picture of a baby to symbolize the beginning of the New Year or she may want to draw something that indicates "newness" to her.

Proceed in the same manner for the remaining months. The two most difficult months may be August and September, which have no major national holidays. A summer scene might be a good choice for August, while September could feature a back-to-school picture.

When the calendar is complete, use paper fasteners or staples to put it all together.

Extension

Help your child go through the calendar and add symbols for major national and religious holidays. You may also want to help her compile a list of significant family dates such as birthdays and anniversaries that she can add to the calendar as appropriate.

This is also a good time to teach your child the "Thirty Days Hath September" mnemonic if she doesn't already know it.

Thirty days hath September,
April, June, and November,
February has twenty-eight alone,
And all the rest have thirty-one;
Except for leap year—that's the time
When February's days are twenty-nine.

Science and

Social Studies

W hen someone asked Thomas Edison why he couldn't accept failure after 10,000 attempts at trying to make a contraption work, Edison replied that he hadn't failed. Instead, he pointed out, he had succeeded in finding 10,000 ways that don't work. If it weren't for Edison's attitude, you'd be reading this section in the dark! That's what science is all about — having ideas and seeing them through. Watch the joy of discovery when your children see the sound of their voices vibrate on a wall or as they watch crystals form from the salt they threw into vinegary water. These are only two of the many activities suggested in this section that delve into the magical world of science.

The social studies activities presented here use play to teach children the spirit of cooperation, sharing, giving, and understanding of others. They provide ample opportunities for children to explore the connections between their own beliefs and actions and that of others. You might want to enrich their exploration by reading stories to them that have originated in different cultures and in different eras of our history. The fact that you take the time to conduct these activities with your children illustrates to them what cooperation, sharing, etc. are all about. You are helping them to realize their special role at home and, by extension, in society at large.

Sounds Good

½ hour +

Sounds are invisible. But you can feel and see sound vibrations. The following experiments with sound will work for the average child as well as one who is hearing-impaired.

Supplies

> Balloon
> Scissors
> Short cardboard tube
> Rubber band
> Small piece of aluminum foil
> Flashlight
> Glue

Directions

Cut off the neck of the balloon and discard it. Stretch the balloon skin tightly over one end of the tube. Use a rubber band to hold it in place. Glue a small piece of foil (about the size of a postage stamp) to the balloon skin. Dim the light in a room. Shine the flashlight on the foil in such a way that it casts a reflection onto a wall. Speak into the open end of the tube. Experiment with short, long, high, low, loud, and quiet sounds. What happens to the spot of light? You can explain to your child that sounds make vibrations. The vibrations travel through the tube, making the balloon skin, and the foil attached to it, vibrate. So the reflected light vibrates, too. Try singing a song or saying a rhyme into the tube.

Extension

(Note: If you have only one balloon, you may want to do

this extension activity before the previous one.) Turn on the radio or cassette/CD player. Hold a blown-up balloon in front of a loudspeaker. Talk about the vibrations made by different kinds of music. Do the vibrations traveling through the balloon feel different? Did you notice that high-pitched sounds create faster vibrations and vice versa?

Piñata Wishes

¾ to 1 hour

Save this activity for a party. Before creating the piñata, explain its origin, i.e., it comes from the Hispanic culture and it was used at celebrations to entertain children and give them gifts.

Supplies

Thin paper bag
Tissue paper or other very light paper, e.g., onionskin
Masking tape or rubber band
Glue
Scissors
Long string
Markers
Lined paper
Candy (preferably sugar-free) or a handmade gift,
    e.g., popcorn necklace

Directions

Help your child write wishes for party guests on lined paper, leaving at least six lines between wishes. (There could be several wishes per guest.) Some examples of wishes are: good health, a call from a friend, happiness. Cut the wishes out, leaving enough blank paper to wrap a candy or gift inside. Put the stuffed "wish" wrappers inside a thin paper bag. Inflate the bag and secure it with tape or a rubber band. Attach a string to the container long enough to hang the piñata from the ceiling when it is completed. Cut a lot of tissue paper into strips about six inches wide. Fold the strips in half. Assemble several layers of these strips and cut a one-inch fringe along the edges. Apply glue sparingly along one side of each strip and attach it to the bag. Start at one end of the bag and continue working in the same direction toward the other side. When done, fluff up the fringes. Hang the piñata low enough for your child to reach. During the party, your child can smash the piñata open with a baseball bat or broom handle. The guests can pick wrappers and read their wishes out loud. Guests can ask your child the reason behind the wishes. Note: older children might have enough strength to break open a piñata made from a cereal box or inflated plastic bag.

Extension

You and your child can create your own party favors. You can make shakers using plastic containers or small boxes.

Fill each container with objects that will rattle around inside, e.g., seeds, pasta, buttons, beans. Decorate the containers with colored paper. For variety, tie a bunch of plastic bottle tops or beads to a string that is attached to the end of a stick.

Over the Rainbow

¼ to ½ hour

Have you ever wished you can find the pot of gold at the end of a rainbow? Discover your child's wishes with this simple activity that fosters thinking in both science and social studies. You will need to do this activity on a sunny day.

Supplies

Small bowl
Water
Small mirror
Sheet of white paper

Directions

Fill the bowl with water and put a mirror into it. Position the bowl so that the sun shines on the mirror. Hold up a sheet of white paper in such a way that a rainbow is reflected from the mirror onto the paper. If you hold the paper very steady, you will see all the rainbow colors.

Ask your child to talk about what he or she thinks is at the end of the rainbow. Is this treasure something good for anyone who finds it? Why? Have your child imagine that three children arrive at the end of the rainbow at different times. Each finds a gift there. One child is your child. One is an orphan. One is a child from a very poor country. What gift did each child receive? What did the child do with the gift? Your child can draw one of the "end of the rainbow" scenarios to illustrate the story.

Extension

Find rainbow colors in different objects made of cut glass (wine glasses, vases, etc.) and jewelry with glassy stones. Hold them up in sunlight and examine the colors.

Carrot Plant

½ hour

The sun gives us light. This light has tremendous power. Plants get their energy to grow from sunlight. Let your child discover the power of the sun with this experiment.

Supplies

Carrot with its leafy shoots intact
Knife
Plastic toothpick or kebob stick
Long string
Water

Directions

Slice off about one to two inches of the leafy end of the carrot. Scoop out the center of the carrot, creating a bowl with a narrow rim. Push the toothpick or stick through the carrot bowl. Loop and tie both ends of a long string to the stick. Hang the carrot plant in front of a sunny window so that the leaves hang down. Fill the carrot bowl with water, topping it up for a few days. Watch the carrot leaves grow upward, toward the light.

Extension

You can demonstrate the need for light with any house plant. Put a plant a little away from a sunny window. Watch the plant leaves twist and turn over time trying to reach the light. If you have a small plant that is not flowering, place it on a sunny window ledge. Water it well. Poke a hole about halfway up on one side of a small box. Cover the plant with the box. In about five days, take the box away. How does the plant look? Why are all the stems bent in one direction?

Bath Boat

½ to ¾ hour

The antics of the Bath Boat will make even the most stubborn child want to take a bath.

Supplies

Plastic bottle with a top
Vinegar
Baking Soda
Tissue paper
Plastic drinking straw
Play dough
Scissors or knife

Directions

Poke a small hole through the bottom of the bottle, close to the edge. Push the straw through the hole, leaving about ½" sticking out. Bend the straw a little toward the edge. Wrap play dough around the straw to keep it secure and to make the bottle airtight. Put some baking soda on tissue paper and roll up the paper. Twist the ends of the paper so that it resembles a tootsie roll wrapper. Pour some vinegar into the bottle. Insert the paper with the soda into the bottle. Put the top on the bottle as quickly as you can. Put the bottle gently into a bathtub full of water and let it go. Watch the boat scoot around the tub.

Extension

Discuss the properties of gas. The Bath Boat is an example. When the vinegar wet the paper, the paper untwisted. The soda and vinegar then mixed together. This created a lot of gas. The gas came out through the plastic straw and pushed the boat. You can view how the gas is formed by using a clear plastic bottle that can be sealed with a cork. Dip the cork into water to make it very wet. Put some baking soda into the bottle. Pour some vinegar inside and quickly cork the bottle. Stand back and wait for the cork to pop.

Heat Conductors

¼ to ½ hour

Your child may have observed that you use a potholder to handle some pots and pans while others do not require a potholder. Here's a simple demonstration that will introduce him to the concept of conductors and, at the same time, reinforce an important safety lesson.

Supplies

Bowl

Hot water

Wooden spoon or other wooden utensil

Metal spoon

Two cooking pans, one with a plastic or wooden handle and one with a metal handle

Potholder

Directions

Fill the bowl with hot water. Have your child insert the wooden spoon into the hot water. Does the spoon feel warm? Now have him insert the metal spoon. Does the metal spoon feel warm? Explain that some materials allow heat to pass through them. These materials are called *conductors*. Which spoon was made of a conductor—the wooden spoon or the metal spoon? Have your child repeat this experiment with other metallic and nonmetallic objects such as paper clips, safety pins, plastic combs, and paper straws. Help him conclude that metals are good conductors while most nonmetallic materials are not.

Extension

Show your child the two pans. Tell him that when you cook you need to use a potholder with one of the pans but not with the other. Can he guess which pan needs a potholder? Why does it need a potholder? Show him the potholder. Ask him if it is a conductor. Explain that materials that do not conduct heat are called *insulators*.

Help your child apply what he's learned to everyday situations. For example, metal connectors on seat belts can get burning hot on a summer day. Metal playground slides can also get perilously hot—proceed with caution!

Seeing Stars

½ hour +

When you combine a little astronomy with arts and crafts, you get an activity that cultivates creativity and stimulates scientific inquiry.

Supplies

Black construction paper
Gummed stars

Directions

Choose a clear, starry night for some family stargazing. Try to point out the Big Dipper or other constellations. If you're up for it, do a little library research beforehand. Ask the librarian to give you a few books that contain myths and legends dealing with constellations. Share these stories with your child. Then have her use the gummed stars and black paper to create her own star picture.

Extension

Once your child has heard a few folk tales concerning constellations, she will enjoy making up her own. Encourage her to write her own story of a constellation. She can dictate it to you and then illustrate it. The black paper and gummed stars can make an attractive book cover.

If your child shows marked interest in the constellations you may also want to suggest that she use her gummed stars to copy established constellation patterns such as the Big Dipper and Orion.

Why Milk?

¼ hour +

Next time your child protests against drinking milk[*], use this simple demonstration to explain why calcium is so important to his growth and development. You may even convince yourself!

Supplies

Slender chicken bone from a cooked chicken (a wishbone or
    wing bone will do)
Enough vinegar to cover the bone
Bowl or jar

---

[*]Many people are allergic to milk and milk products. If your child is one of them, you can use this activity to "defend" other foods that are calcium rich, such as spinach, tofu, and almonds.

Directions

Explain to your child that bones need calcium to be strong and hard. This is also true of chicken bones. To demonstrate what happens when bones are deprived of calcium, place the chicken bone into the vinegar for a few days. Since vinegar dissolves calcium, when the bone is eventually removed, it's soft and rubbery.

Extension

Calcium is just one of many vital nutrients our bodies need. Help your child investigate what other vitamins and minerals our bodies need and what roles they play in keeping us healthy. A good book on nutrition should get you started. Ask your children's librarian for recommendations but look the books over carefully before you choose. Many people disagree about certain nutritional issues and you'll want to pick a book that conforms with your own point of view.

Another good way to follow up this activity is to have your child cut out magazine pictures of foods that are rich in specific vitamins and minerals. Ask her to divide these pictures into categories and mount them on a chart.

Patriotic Flowers

½ hour +

Most plants have tiny tubes in their stems and leaves which carry water and nutrients throughout the plant. Use this simple activity to demonstrate the concept of a vascular system and to brighten your home for the Fourth of July.

Supplies

White carnations (as many as you want to use)
Two small vases or tall cups
Red food coloring
Blue food coloring

Directions

Explain that you are going to use the flowers to make holiday decorations. Put a drop or two of food coloring into each of the vases and add water. Ask your child if he can think of a way to use the food coloring to make the carnations turn red and blue for the Fourth of July. If he suggests soaking the flowers in the food coloring, point out that the flowers would droop and lose their beauty. Explain that the stem of each flower has tiny tubes in it. These tubes can carry water up to the flower. Have your child place a flower in each vase and set the vases in a sunny location. In a day or two, the carnations should begin to gain color.

Extension

Naturally, other colors can be used for different occasions: green for St. Patrick's Day, orange for Halloween, and so on. You can also create multicolored carnations by slitting their stems and placing each half into a different colored water.

You may be familiar with the "grand-daddy" of this demonstration: the celery stalk maneuver. Celery also soaks up food coloring and it's easy for children to handle.

Butterflies Are Free

½ hour +

The transformation of a caterpillar into a butterfly is a rare and astonishing sight that few of us ever see. With this simple activity, you and your child can become two of a privileged few.

Supplies

Large glass jar with a lid
Sharp tool for poking holes in the lid
Caterpillars
Leaves

Directions

Choose a nice September or October day to get this activity started. Poke many tiny holes in the lid of the jar so that air can get in. Have your child go out in the park or your yard and collect two or three caterpillars. The caterpillars should be put into the jar along with a few leaves and a stick. Put a few drops of water on the leaves. Put the lid on the jar. Set the jar outside on a windowsill or on your patio. Have your child feed the caterpillars fresh leaves every day. As the temperature drops, your child will notice that the caterpillars stop eating the leaves. If the caterpillar is a moth caterpillar, it will start to spin a cocoon. If it is a butterfly caterpillar, it will begin to get harder and change into a chrysalis. (A cocoon is a silky object while a chrysalis is a hard, protective shell.) Some time later, possibly when spring arrives, moths or butterflies will hatch.

Extension

Accurate record-keeping is an essential part of good scientific research. You may want to help your child set up a progress chart on which he can keep track of exactly when the caterpillar stopped eating, how they looked at weekly intervals, and when they emerged from their cocoons or chrysalises.

This activity can be enhanced by a trip to the library for some books about caterpillars and butterflies. If you're lucky, you may be able to identify the specimens you collected.

If you haven't got time to go to the library, you may want to explain to your child that butterflies are useful insects because they carry pollen and also serve as an inspiration to many a craftsperson or artist. On the other hand, many caterpillars are harmful, destroying millions of dollars in crops all over the world.

Full of Air

¼ hour

Since air is invisible (except in our smoggier cities) children usually find it hard to believe that air takes up space. Here's a simple demonstration you can use to illustrate this important scientific principle.

Supplies

Small piece of paper
Empty drinking glass
Deep bowl or small bucket of water

Directions

Wad up the piece of paper and place it in the bottom of the glass. The paper should be large enough to remain wedged in the bottom of the glass when the glass is turned upside down. Explain to your child that you plan to plunge the glass, open end down, into the bucket of water. Ask her to predict whether or not the paper will get wet. Once she has made her prediction, plunge the glass straight down into the water. Remove the glass and ask her to take out the wad of paper. The paper will be dry.

Explain that although the glass seemed to be empty it was actually full of air. The air shielded the paper and prevented the water from wetting the wad.

Extension

Your child can actually "see" the air in the glass if you repeat this experiment and tip the glass slightly. You'll both notice that the air will escape in the form of bubbles, allowing water to enter the glass.

Salty Crystals

½ hour +

There's nothing more satisfying than growing something from a handful of ordinary ingredients. In this activity, as the water evaporates, salt crystals begin to grow on the rocks.

Supplies

Porous rocks or coal

Bowl (soup or cereal)

> Warm water
> Salt
> Tablespoon
> Vinegar

Directions

With your child, find small stones or rocks with lots of holes in them. Fill a bowl halfway with water. Add salt and stir. Keep adding one tablespoon at a time. Stir thoroughly after each spoonful of vinegar. Stir it all up. Put the rocks into the bowl—the more you have, the better it works. Stack the rocks so that some are above the water level. In about 24 hours, salt crystals will start to grow on the rocks.

Extension

Explain to your child that the vinegar plays an important part in this experiment. It cleanses the rocks and makes it easier for the water to flow through the pores. If possible, enrich this activity by taking your child on a nature walk to look for crystalline rocks. A pocket magnifier will help you examine rocks for crystals.

Fossil Foolery

½ hour +

Fossils are a wonderful window into the past. Here's a recipe for do-it-yourself fossils that will help your child understand how fossils are formed.

Supplies

Clay or play clay (see recipe on p. 180)

Disposable aluminum foil cake pan (round, square, or rectangular)

Plaster of paris

Fossil candidates: anything you want to make into a fossil—
for example, a shell or a chicken bone

Directions

Have your child make a layer of play dough or clay on the bottom of the cake pan. Instruct her to press her fossil candidate into the clay. Help her follow the directions on the plaster of paris and pour the plaster mix into the pan. Let the plaster harden for at least ten hours (overnight is best). When the plaster is thoroughly hard and dry, have her pull away the cake pan and voilà! Her fossil is done.

Extension

Your child may enjoy learning a bit about the scientists who hunt and study fossils. Called paleontologists, these scientists usually search in sedimentary rock (rock that was formed from layers of small particles over thousands of years) for the remains of animals and plants from different times in Earth's history. Once found, the fossils are cleaned and studied in laboratories and museums. Paleontologists compare them with other fossils and with living plants and animals. Paleontologists learn a great deal about Earth's past from this study.

Fossils are on display in most natural history museums and can also be found in your own neighborhood. Some museums, such as the Page Museum in Los Angeles, let visitors watch technicians and scientists clean bones and other fossils. Your nearest natural history museum may be willing to set up a demonstration for your child and a group of friends. Don't be shy, it never hurts to ask!

How Does Your Garden Grow?

½ hour +

This activity will introduce your child to some basics about plant growth and development. It's simple to do and decorative too.

Supplies

Four small, healthy plants in separate pots
(these can be grown from seed—radish seed sprouts and grows relatively quickly; styrofoam coffee cups can be used as pots)
Closet
Water

Directions

Tell your child that plants need rich soil in which to grow. Point out that gardeners often add nutrients to their soil to improve their plants. Ask your child if he knows what else plants need to grow. Ask him if plants need light and water. How can he prove it? Tell him to place one of the pots in a dark closet and one on a sunny windowsill. Have him water each plant equally for several days and check them daily. What happens to the plant in the closet?

Next, ask your child how he can prove that plants need water. Help him set up an experiment in which he places two healthy plants side by side in a sunny location but only waters one. What happens?

Extension

The stems of almost all green plants grow upward. This way the leaves stay free of soil and other debris and sunlight can reach them without obstacles. If a green plant is tipped on its side its leaves will usually bend upward. This remarkable tendency is called *tropism.* You can demonstrate this tendency to your child by tipping one of your radish plants on its side. What happens after several days?

An Herb Garden—Egg Carton Style

½ hour +

Herbs are easy to grow, live inside year round, and are a wonderful first crop for young gardeners. This activity may well spark a lifelong interest in botany or agriculture.

Supplies

> Egg carton
> Nail
> Pebbles
> Potting soil
> Herb seeds—choose family favorites such as dill, basil, or parsley
> Tray
> Full watering can
> Small clay or plastic pots

Directions

Show your child how to fill up the egg carton: first puncture a small hole with a nail in each egg cup for drainage. Then add a few small pebbles, some soil, and two or three seeds to each egg cup. Sprinkle with dirt to cover seeds. Water and place in a sunny window (on a tray to avoid a mess). Make sure the egg carton is kept moist and when the seedlings have sprouted—two to three inches—transplant to clay pots, repeating procedure of pebbles at bottom and additional earth above. (To transplant, tap seedlings from each egg cup, being careful to keep a ball of dirt around roots.) Keep herbs moist and in a sunny window for year-round yield.

Extension

Encourage your child to use and develop his senses of smell and taste by having a "blindfold" herb test. Can he identify the herbs you grow by just tasting or smelling them? Point out that blind people often have heightened senses of smell and taste because they rely on them heavily for information about the world around them.

You may also want to mention to your child that, in many cultures, herbs are used for cosmetic and healing purposes. If you're lucky enough to live near an Asian neighborhood, take a trip to an old-fashioned Asian pharmacy for a firsthand look at herbal remedies.

In some cultures, people believe that certain herbs have specific qualities. You and your child might enjoy exploring these "personalities" at your local library.

Wild Bird Feeder

¼ to ½ hour

Kids are amused to learn that birds too love peanut butter. Once your kids make this very simple wild bird feeder, they'll have many a meal watching their feathered friends also "at table." This activity may lead to a lifetime hobby of bird watching and study of ornithology.

Supplies

> Cord
> Large pinecone
> Peanut butter
> Spoon
> Waxed paper
> Birdseed

Directions

Tie cord to top of the pinecone and then use a spoon to spread peanut butter on the cone's petals. Next, roll the pinecone on waxed paper that has been covered with birdseed. Hang your wild bird feeder from a tree and watch the birds arrive for supper.

Extension

Learning about different kinds of birds and their habits is the natural outgrowth of owning a bird feeder. Start with the simple, everyday birds your feeder attracts; your child can keep a "log" of the birds she sees. (A library book on birds will help her identify them.) Talk about how birds live. Where do they live? Do they stay all winter or fly south from your location? When do they return? What are their feeding habits? What's in birdseed anyway? Do all birds eat worms? Pretty soon you will be as hooked as your kids—bird watching, and learning, is family fun.

Autumn Placemats

1 hour +

This fun-to-do craft project will help your child appreciate some of the changes that take place as summer gives way to fall. When the project is complete, memories of early October will be present for months to come as your child enjoys breakfast on her autumn placemat.

Supplies

Autumn leaves
Scissors
Heavy construction paper
White craft glue
Waxed paper
Heavy books
Paintbrush
Clear varnish or liquid plastic finish

Directions

Take a nature walk with your child and point out that many of the leaves on the trees have changed colors. Ask questions that will help her focus on seasonal changes. What color were the leaves in summer? What will happen to the leaves in winter? What happens to the trees in spring? Which season is the warmest? Coldest? Most colorful? In which season does school begin? When does school end? When is Christmas or Chanukah? As you walk, can she gather a collection of colorful leaves to take home for her placemats.

Let your child cut construction paper into placemat-sized rectangles. Instruct her to squeeze glue onto the veined, or underneath side, of autumn leaves and arrange them in attractive patterns on the construction paper. Press firmly down and cover with sheets of waxed paper. Place heavy books on top of the waxed paper. When thoroughly dry, peel off waxed paper and brush on a coat of varnish or liquid plastic. Let dry and varnish two more times, allowing placemat to dry between coats.

Extension

A trip to your local library should yield a selection of nature guides that your child can use to identify common trees in your area. Go on a nature hike and see how many you can name. As you go on your hike you may also want to explain to your child that some trees lose their leaves in the winter and are called "deciduous trees," while others keep their leaves during the winter and are called "evergreens." In the fall, deciduous trees are the ones that start to change color. How many deciduous trees can you spot? Evergreens?

Rainy Day Fun

½ hour +

This activity can turn a gray, rainy day into a special science learning treat for your child. It is also useful for reinforcing measurement skills.

Supplies

Globe or map of the world
Glass jar (a slender olive jar would be best)
Ruler
Colored nail polish
Funnel
Empty coffee can

Directions

Explain to your child that different parts of the world get different amounts of rainfall. Tropical areas get a huge amount of rain, temperate zones get a medium amount, and deserts get very little. As you explain, point out corresponding areas on the globe or map.

Tell him a little about meteorologists, who keep track of how much rain an area gets by measuring it with a tool called a "rain gauge." Does he want to make his own? Hold the ruler next to the jar and help him use the nail polish to mark off two inches in quarter-inch increments. Have him place the funnel in the jar and put the jar inside the coffee can (the coffee can will keep the jar from being knocked down by the wind or heavy rainfall).

Let your child put on his rain gear and place the coffee can gauge in an unsheltered area in your yard, balcony, or on your windowsill. Have him check the gauge periodically. What was the total rainfall? How does your total compare with the weatherperson's total on the evening news? Why does it differ? (The weather station's gauge is probably a different diameter than your jar and is marked off in more precise and frequent intervals.)

Extension

Help your child make a grid for a bar graph to keep track of daily rainfall over a period of a month. How many days did it rain? Which day had the most rainfall? Which rainy day had the least rainfall?

Get a book from the library that compares average annual rainfall in major U.S. cities. Where would your child prefer to live, Seattle or Tucson?

Describe or read the story of Noah's Ark to your child. Ask your librarian to help you find other stories about rain. An excellent choice for four-year-olds would be *Umbrella* by Taro Yashima, Viking Books.

Hug a Tree

½ hour

This is a nature/thinking activity. It forces a child to use all of her senses and reveals to her the amazing individuality of nature.

Supplies

Wooded area

Blindfold

Directions

Blindfold your child and lead her to a tree. Help her explore the tree with her hands and face. "What does it feel like? Does it have a lot of bark? Is it fat? Thin? Can you hug it all the way around? How does it feel when you rub your face on it?" After this "blind" examination, lead your child back to her starting point. Use a slightly zigzag way back to confuse her. Then remove the blindfold. Ask her if she can find "her" tree. Now you take a turn.

Extension

Bring along a camera, a magnifying glass, and binoculars. Take a picture of your child next to her tree. Let her use the magnifying glass to explore it up close. Are there insects on it? Are there signs of birds or any other animals? Take a follow-up trip to the library and find a forestry guide to identify the tree.

The World by the Tail

½ hour

This variation on Pin the Tail on the Donkey is an excellent way to introduce your child to maps and how they are organized. Use the extension activity to teach a bit of world geography, too.

Supplies

Large map of the world
Colored construction paper
Tape or push pins
Blindfold
Two or more players

Directions

Show the children the map and explain that the blue areas indicate water and the other colored areas indicate land. Cut a house shape out of the paper and pin or tape this to the map at the approximate location that indicates your home. Cut airplane shapes from the paper. Each player should get a plane of a different color. Each player is blindfolded and spins around three or four times. Then he tries to place his plane as far from home as possible—but he must end up on *land*. If you want to, you can make this into a competitive game by awarding points for each time a player lands on land.

Extension

For more sophisticated players who are ready to learn a bit more about world geography, add the following: when a player lands his plane, name the country for him and, if possible, tell him a bit about the country's climate. Then ask, "If you were going on a trip to this country, what would you pack?"

People and Places in Your Neighborhood

½ to 1 hour

Kids are intrigued by things that grown-ups use. A map is a good example. On car trips, they'll look at the map and wonder what relation it bears to the roads you are taking. And while road maps may be too difficult for young kids, their neighborhoods are just the right size for a beginner's map. This activity will introduce your child to some basic map skills and provide you both with an opportunity to do an armchair exploration of your neighborhood.

Supplies
Pencil and paper
Square piece of muslin or white cotton (size optional)
Felt tip pen
Felt scraps

Directions
Using pencil and paper, sketch out the major landmarks of your town or neighborhood—the school, post office, fire department, supermarket, etc. Help your child put them on a plausible north-south footing. Then add more personal landmarks—these might include Grandma's house, a friend's house, the toy store, whatever places in your neighborhood are important to your child. When the sketch is complete,

duplicate it with felt pen on your square piece of cotton. Fashion landmarks out of felt and glue to fabric. Hang the map on the wall of your kitchen or your child's room.

Extension

Cartography, or the science of maps, can fascinate children. When you travel, indicate the places on a map you will go. Point out, again on a map, where friends and relatives were born or grew up. Pinpoint several states on a U.S. map and describe their location in terms of East Coast, West Coast, Midwest, etc. Explain how the sun rises in the east and sets in the west and then play versions of "east-west" with your kids. Is that tree in the east or west? That house? Purchase an inexpensive compass and explain how it works. Pretty soon everyone in your family will have a fine sense of direction!

Motor Development and Self-Awareness

Two-year-olds like to creep, lug, tug, drag, fetch, and carry things. They enjoy taking things apart, putting things back, and making a mess. Between the ages of two and five they want to run, jump, skip, and play with objects that challenge their strength and coordination. Their natural instincts for movement make it ideal for you to try out activities in this section that develop both locomotor skills (walking, jumping) and non-locomotor skills (twisting, folding). You can provide additional opportunities by:

- Having them invent movements, e.g., "How many ways can you move your arms?"
- Urging them to expand on a movement, for example, "Can you show me how you walk in a parade? Upstairs? Downhill?"
- Relating a movement to rhythm, for example, "Can you clap every time you hear a rhyme?"
- Asking them to act out a story or an idea, for example, "How did the mice run up the clock?"

As children acquire motor skills, they develop a sense of self at the same time. They are exploring self-esteem, values, goals, and feelings. They are constantly asking "Why?" in an attempt to understand who they are. Take the time to help them examine their likes and dislikes, their strengths and weakness, and their potential. The activities in this section provide fun activities that help children come to an understanding of exactly who they are and what they are capable of.

Stackable Castle

½ to ¾ hour

At one time or another we all tried to stack playing cards into a structure that was free-standing. Getting the balance just right and coordinating your movements so that the cards wouldn't fall over was no easy task. However, there was sheer satisfaction when the chore was accomplished. Here's a stacking activity that results in more joy than frustration.

Supplies

Construction paper
Scissors
Masking tape

Directions

Tape construction paper cylinders of various diameters and heights. Cut two slits halfway through each cylinder. Interlock the cylinders by fitting the slits together. When your child is pleased with the architectural design, help him/her to cut square grooves at the top of the cylinders that sit at the top of the structure. The finished castle should be so strong that it can be lifted by a turret without falling apart.

Extension

Ask your child to tell you about the people who live in the castle. Talk about the books you have read about kingdoms with castles. Can your child make up a story about him-or-herself living or visiting the castle?

Skittle Bowling

½ to 1 hour

What do you do with toys that are no longer interesting to your child? Here's a solution. After playing with a hand-made bowling toy, discover ways to recycle it for other creative purposes.

Supplies

> Six plastic bottles with plastic lids
> Sand
> Powder paint (optional)
> Funnel
> Ball

Directions

Fill each bottle half full with sand. For a colorful display, you might want to mix powder paint into the sand. Seal the bottle tightly. Find a level, hard surface in the house or outside. Take away breakable objects from the area. Line up the bottles in the shape of a triangle, with three bottles in the back row, two in the middle, and one in the first row. Illustrate to your child how to roll, not throw, the ball along the floor toward the skittle pins. Explain that the object of the sport is to knock down all the pins.

Extension

When it's time to recycle the skittle pins, use papier-mâché and collage materials on the sand-filled bottles to create robots, dolls, vases, or animals. Your child can give these creations as gifts.

My Personal Crest

½ hour +

Discuss with your child how in the old days, families and individuals had crests to symbolize their personal traits. In the old days, like in King Arthur's time, crests were mounted on castles, on riding gear, on clothes, and other objects to indicate who owned these things. You might want to show your child pictures of U.S. emblems (another word for crests), such as the Great Shield.

Supplies

Paper
Markers or crayons
Ruler
Scissors

Directions

Draw the outline of the shape for a crest. Divide the crest shape into six parts. In part one, draw a self-portrait. In part two, draw a favorite activity, for example, baseball.

In part three, draw a picture of your house. In part four, draw a picture of your pet or favorite animal. In part five, draw a picture of your parents or closest relatives. In part six, draw a picture of what you want to be when you grow up. Cut the crest out and tape it to the door of your room.

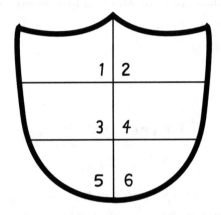

Extension

Create a family crest in the same way, or you can create a family banner using a large piece of paper or fabric.

My Community

¾ hour+

Is your child aware of the different levels of human relationships? There's the home, neighborhood, town, country, and world. Before he/she can grasp large community relationships, start with the immediate neighborhood.

Supplies

> Several small boxes or angular containers
> Paint
> Glue
> Colored paper
> Masking tape
> Plastic or formica table

Directions

Paint boxes and paste shapes onto boxes to resemble build-ings in your neighborhood, for example, your place of wor-ship, your home, the post office. Using tape, lay out a grid of streets on a table. Place the structures on the grid. Discuss the concept of a community: What kind of people work in the area (doctor, bank teller, etc.)? What kind of buildings are there (school, church, apartment building)? What can people do to make their neighborhood pretty (lights on trees, flower pots on sidewalks)?

Extension

Complete the neighborhood by adding details. Use twigs and tissue paper for trees. Painted popsicle sticks can be traffic lights. Tiny cartons can become mailboxes. To experiment with ideas of distance, viewpoint, overlapping, and size, have your child view the community from different angles.

Basketball Star

¼ to ½ hour

Here are three rhythmic activities using a ball, a fun way to improve coordination. On a rainy day, you can do these exercises at home or in the garage.

Supplies

Three or four low-back chairs
(for smaller children, you can use boxes)
Small to medium-size bouncing ball
Trash can

Directions

Line up the chairs or boxes in a straight line, with ample room for movement between them. Place a trash can at the end of the row, up against a wall. In the first exercise, the child can skip or jog while dribbling the ball around the perimeter of the row of obstacles. Next, the child can skip or jog around and between the obstacles while bouncing the ball, shoot it into the trash can, and skip back. Now, standing behind the chair or box closest to the trash can, see if your child can throw the ball over the obstacle and into the can. Move one chair or box further and try again. Do the same with all obstacles in the row.

Extension

Talk about how a ball is used in different games and what it can do. Does your child have a favorite ball game? What other equipment is needed to play the game? What is the purpose of the game: to shoot the ball into a basket, to hit it over a net, to win, or to have fun, etc.? How many sports does your child know about that use a ball (e.g., handball)? What do these balls look like? Draw them.

Kick It

¼ to ½ hour

In recent years many child development specialists have suggested that motor coordination and early reading ability are interconnected. In broad terms, they believe that children with good coordination are better able to process and accept information. This simple activity is excellent for developing motor skills and mental concentration.

Supplies

Two volleyball-size balls
Two or more players (if there are more children, you'll need more balls)

Directions

Kick It is basically a race. Set up starting and finishing lines. To win, the children must kick their balls as they make their way toward the finish line. The winner is the first child who has himself and his ball over the line. Players may not touch the balls with their hands.

Extension

If your child is ready for a bigger challenge, try substituting different kinds of balls. A small tennis ball or an ordinary football will make Kick It an even more exciting race.

Finger Lickin' Good

½ hour

Many bright children have trouble with handwriting. For whatever reason, their fine motor coordination is not as advanced as their thinking skills. Luckily, in most cases a little practice goes a long way. Here's a great activity to make the tedious a whole lot more tasty.

Supplies
Instant pudding
Milk

Directions
With your child's assistance, follow the directions on the pudding package to make pudding. Spread out a glob of pudding on a piece of waxed paper. (Prepare two pieces of paper, one for you and one for your child.) Use the pudding like fingerpaint to print a letter with your index finger. Ask your child to trace the same letter on her pudding palate. Go through the entire alphabet, devoting more time to letters that are especially difficult for your child. Naturally, you can expect your pudding artist to lick her "brush" after each letter.

Extension
If you prefer, this activity also can be done with flavored gelatin mix (not prepared but dry), whipped cream, or pureed fruit. Another fun way to practice letter formation is by "writing" letters in clay. Your child might enjoy creating a clay name plaque for himself or a relative. Once dry, the plaque can be coated with white construction glue. This will

give it an even surface which, when dry, can be colored with magic markers.

One in a Million

½ hour +

Here's an activity that will develop perceptual skills and give children a taste of their own uniqueness.

Supplies

Number 2 or other soft-lead pencil
Several sheets of paper
Transparent tape
Pocket magnifier

Directions

Rub the pencil (on its side) on a sheet of paper. Rub the pencil until you have a very thick coating of lead. Press your child's index finger on the black coating and have him make a fingerprint on the sticky side of a piece of transparent tape. Attach the fingerprinted tape to a piece of paper. Have your child write his name under his print. Now use the pencil again to make a new coating. Ask your child to make your fingerprint and write your name under it. Suggest that he catalog each family member in this way. Have him examine each fingerprint, and discuss how each one is different. Point out that no two people in the world have the same fingerprints.

Extension

Explain to your child how law enforcement agencies use

fingerprints to identify people. Create a simple detective game for him to play in your home. Show him an unlabeled fingerprint and ask him to compare it to the family fingerprint catalog he made earlier. Challenge him to guess whose fingerprint it is.

Chopstick Race

¼ to ½ hour

Fine motor skills are essential for good handwriting. This tummy-tickling race will refine your child's small motor skills and give her an opportunity to learn how to use chopsticks.

Supplies

Two or more sets of chopsticks

Four or more bowls

Small finger foods such as walnuts, popcorn, marshmallows, radishes, cherry tomatoes

Two or more players

Directions

Show your child how to hold the chopsticks. Give her and any other players a chance to experiment picking things up with them. (If the proper way to use the chopsticks seems too difficult for your group, allow the children to use them any way they please as long as they do not touch the food with their fingers.)

Place an even number of items in two or more bowls. Give one bowl to each player. Give each player an additional empty bowl. On your signal, players must use their chopsticks to transfer the items to their empty bowls. The first player to move all her items wins the race. When the race is over, players can eat the playing pieces. (Note: If your child is competing against an adult, give the adult twice or three times as many items to move to the empty bowl.)

Extension

If your child is ready to take on a more difficult task, try substituting marbles for the food items. It takes exceptionally fine motor control and concentration to lift marbles with chopsticks. (Naturally, marbles cannot be eaten.)

Shades of the Past—Making Silhouettes

½ hour

Children are fascinated by shadows. When they make silhouettes, they not only capture a shadow but they also revive an old-fashioned skill. This activity will give your child valuable fine motor practice.

Supplies

Masking tape
Four sheets of paper, two light and two dark
Flashlight or slide projector
Pencil
Scissors
White craft glue

Directions

Tape a large piece of light colored paper to a blank wall. Have your child sit sideways in front of the paper. Point a flashlight or the beam of the slide projector at your child. Move your child, or the flashlight, until his shadow in profile is clearly outlined on the paper. With your pencil, carefully trace his profile onto your paper and then have him cut out the silhouette and glue it to a second, larger size dark-colored background paper. Next, trade places, and have him make your silhouette.

Extension

This project offers a good chance to introduce your child to our nation's past. Explain, for example, how silhouettes were used as a quick way to take someone's picture, the way a snapshot is used today. Discuss, too, what makes them different from a painting of a person. Would he like to record all his family in silhouette?

Self-Portrait

½ to 1 hour

The development of a positive self-image is one of the most important milestones in a child's growth. This simple activity is a preschool and kindergarten favorite that will give you insight into your child's perception of herself and, at the same time, promote her self-esteem.

Supplies

Large sheet of brown wrapping paper, at least as long as your child
Pencil
Crayons or felt tip markers

Directions

Have your child stretch herself out on the brown paper. Then trace her outline on the paper with a pencil. Once you have traced her outline, she can fill in the rest with crayons or markers. Suggest that she draw her face to reflect how she feels (happy, sad, angry, and so on) and to dress herself in her favorite kind of clothes. As she colors her portrait, discuss some of the things she fills in. Is her hair curly or straight? Are her eyes round or more oval? Does she have any special features that she's proud of? Are there any things about herself she'd like to change?

Extension

Another way to build self-esteem is to have a family "cheer-leading" session. Sit in a circle with as many family members as you can gather (siblings and extended family members are most welcome here) and choose one family member as the first "star" of the session. Take turns saying at least two nice things about the "star." Warn everyone in advance that no sarcastic or mean comments will be tolerated.

Makeup Mirrors

½ hour +

Most children love to "ham it up" in front of a mirror. This activity is a natural for developing creativity and self-esteem.

Supplies

Cold cream

Cornstarch

Water
Food coloring
Several bowls or cups
Measuring spoons
Large mirror
Tissues

Directions

Help your child create his own stage makeup and use it to act out a favorite story. For each color, mix one tablespoon of cold cream, two teaspoons of cornstarch, one teaspoon of water, and just a few drops of food coloring. Show him how to apply your makeup and stand in front of the mirror. You can act out a favorite story or your own story. When you want to change characters, wipe off your makeup with a tissue and create a new face.

Extension

Ask your child: How could you make your face look old, sad, tired, happy, scary, etc.? What other items could you use to get into character? (Old scarves, hats, glasses, and even frilly lingerie make great costumes.)

At the Hop

½ hour

As we've mentioned before, many early childhood educators have hypothesized a link between muscular coordination and learning readiness. This easy-to-do activity is lots of fun and will help your child develop his hopping ability.

If this seems relatively unimportant to you, take note that most nursery schools include hopping as a milestone on their developmental checklists.

Supplies

Ten sticks, about ten to twelve inches long

Directions

Place the sticks in a column like the rungs of a ladder. The sticks should be about ten inches apart. The object of the activity is to hop over the sticks without touching them. When your child hops over the last stick, he must reach down and pick it up (while staying on one foot). Then he hops back to the beginning, places the stick in a "finished" pile, and begins again. When all the sticks are in the finished pile, the activity is over. If at any point during the hopping he touches a stick with his foot or places two feet on the ground, he must start at the beginning again.

Extension

This activity can easily be adapted as a competitive game with two or more players taking turns. If a player touches a stick or places both feet on the ground, his turn ends and the next child goes. When this game is played with two or more players, sticks are not placed in a finished pile. Each player keeps track of what stick he is up to, just as children do when they play hopscotch.

Paper Doll Capers

½ to 1 hour

Preschool and kindergarten educators frequently assess young children by their ability to identify and properly assign body parts. This activity will not only hone your child's fine motor skills, it will also reinforce his body part awareness.

Supplies

Heavyweight white drawing paper
String
White craft glue
Crayons or colored felt tip markers
Scissors

Directions

Have your child draw the outline of a person on the white paper. Tell him to make the outline large and to omit individual fingers or toes. (Explain that these will be filled in later.) Cut a length of string long enough to wrap around the entire body outline. Have your child dip the string into the glue and carefully press the string down along the body outline. When the glue dries, cut out the "doll" by cutting carefully just outside the string. (The string holds the doll stiff.) Now, he can color in the details. He should add eyes, ears, nose, mouth, hair, hands and fingers, feet, toes, and other body parts, as well as clothes.

Extension

This technique can also be used to create many other different kinds of shapes and objects. Flowers, geometric shapes, animals, and a wide variety of things can be fashioned with string and glue.

Shadow Drama

¼ to ½ hour

This activity does double duty: it enhances creative thinking and provides practice in motor coordination.

Supplies

Flashlight or bright lamp

Blank wall

Directions

In an otherwise darkened room shine the light on the wall. Place your hand between the light and the wall and create shadow figures or animals. You and your child can experiment until you have figured out how to make two or three different things. Using these items (or more), start to tell a story. Have your child join in so that you are "shadow-acting" together.

Extension

If possible, visit your local library or quality bookstore and get a copy of author Remy Charlip's marvelous shadow play book, *Doctor, Doctor.* Not only does it tell the humorous story of a young boy who swallows just about everything but the kitchen sink, it also includes instructions for performing one's own shadow play. (Remy Charlip also wrote *Fortunately, Unfortunately*, another classic for children in this age range.)

Obstacle Fun

½ hour

Obstacle courses are fun to run and also refine a child's motor coordination skills.

Supplies
Common backyard and household objects

Directions
Set up your own obstacle course in your backyard or basement. Old automobile tires make a great starting point. Line them up two by two so that children have to step nimbly from one pair to the next. Follow the tires with a home-made balance beam—a board firmly secured to two wooden blocks or clay bricks. (Whatever you use, be careful not to elevate the board too high. The board does not have to be high off the ground to be a challenging balance activity.) Follow the beam with a climbing challenge: a ladder that leads to a playhouse, a backyard slide, a staircase to the second floor of your house, or a hilly area are all good for this section of the course. Finish your obstacle course with a crawling challenge: a tunnel constructed from old appliance cartons or a sheet suspended low over the ground both make excellent crawling tunnels.

Extension
Define the word *obstacle* for your child and discuss its meaning in terms of her own goals. Is there something she really wants to do or have that she doesn't know how to obtain? Help her outline the obstacles to her success and assess whether and how they are surmountable.

Problem-solving is an important ability that children gain only through practice. The more practice you can give your child in developing this important skill, the better prepared your child will be for her future. Next time you or your child are faced with a problem, even a simple one like which cookies to buy, solve it together using these simple decision-making steps:

1. What are the possible choices?
2. What are the good points and bad points about each?
3. Choose the best solution for you.
4. Act on your decision, assess its success later.

First Up

¼ hour

Are you tired of eeny-meeny-miney-mowing your way into a fair solution for picking which child goes first? Try this parent-tested alternative.

Supplies

None

Directions

Two people face each other, holding one hand behind their backs. In unison, they count aloud to three. On three, each person takes the hidden hand and thrusts it out in one of these configurations:

A fist

A flat palm

Two fingers in the sign of a V

The fist is called *rock*. The palm is *paper*. The fingers are called *scissors*. Every time there is a combination of two, one can beat the other. Scissors cuts paper. Paper covers up the rock. The rock can crush the scissors. Children learn this routine very quickly—and love it. (As a plus, you get a fun way to stop the whining about who goes first!)

Extension

Challenge your child to come up with other fair ways to choose who goes first. If your child needs help, bring out a deck of cards and explain that they can be useful in devising a new method. Demonstrate by suggesting that the person who picks the highest card will go first. How else can the cards be used to choose who goes first?

Winter Count

½ hour

Ever notice how even a five-year-old wants to know "What was I like when I was a baby?" Or "What did I do before I went to nursery school?" "What was our other house like?" You can help her answer these questions and others by doing what the Native American Indians did. Keep a "winter count"—a life record in pictures. This activity is good for language development and also encourages creative self-expression.

Supplies

Long sheet of brown construction paper

Poster paint in bright colors

Directions

A winter count is simple. It starts with a discussion. Ask your child to describe the important events in her life—the day she got her dog, or started school, or made a special friend, and so on. Then help her put these events into sequence, starting with the earliest. Now ask her to draw a series of pictures that will represent these events (a dog, the school, her friend, etc.). As new important days occur, she will want to add them to her winter count. What fun to review the record when she is older!

Extension

A winter count is a natural way for your child to share thoughts and feelings with you. It can also be an opportunity to learn more about the Native American Indians. Explain to your child how the Indians measured time by the passage of each winter. A winter count depicted the major events in their lives over a year's time. These events—perhaps a big battle or a new chief, illness or a plea for rain—were drawn on the walls of caves and on smooth rocks. We can still find them throughout our land, and they are reproduced in books. Get a book of these cave pictures and compare our lives with the lives the Indians described in these paintings. How are they alike? Different?

"Formal" Dining

¼ to 1 hour

Children love company meals and enjoy playing a part in the preparations. Here's an activity that will keep them busy while you're in the kitchen *and* develop their creativity and fine motor skills. It will also introduce them to semiotics (the science of symbols).

Supplies

> List of guests
> Large blank index cards
> Assorted colored markers
> Assorted stickers (optional)

Directions

Give your child the list of guests, delegating the task of making place cards for the dinner table. Show him how to fold the index cards in half so that they stand up on their own. Help him decide how he is going to decorate the cards. Is this a holiday dinner? If it's Christmas, perhaps a small tree on each card would be appropriate. For Chanukah, a menorah or dreidel; for Thanksgiving, a turkey or ear of corn; and so forth.

As you discuss the possibilities, introduce the word "symbol" to your child and explain its meaning. If he wishes to use a variety of symbols on his cards, so much the better, as long as they make sense. Once your child has decided on his symbols, draw a line on each card for him to use as a guide for printing the guests' names.

Extension

If you're making an ethnic meal, help your child develop symbols for the nationality. National flags can be found in most encyclopedias and some of them are easy to reproduce (for example, Italy, Japan, and Nigeria all have very simple flags).

Another way to supplement this activity is to take the ethnic theme a few steps further. For example, if you're cooking a French meal, why not teach your child the words to "Frère Jacques"? A Mexican meal might be accompanied by an exhibition of the Mexican Hat Dance, and so forth. Most children welcome the opportunity to perform and your adult guests will enjoy this very special entertainment.

If you have time, a trip to the library will enhance this activity tremendously. You and your child can check out ethnic records to accompany your dinner and research ethnic customs, setting the table and planning the menu accordingly.

Art and

Creativity

Children love art! They do it for the sheer pleasure it gives them. You'll find that they will be eager to participate in the activities in this section. The activities provide opportunities for your children to manipulate, organize, experiment, perceive relationships in their environment, understand the creative process, and discover the diversity of artistic expression.

Encourage your children's creative efforts. Compliment them often. Never label their art as "wrong." If a child paints a cow purple, that's just his/her interpretation of it. My favorite art teacher always said, "There's no such thing as bad art, only unresolved design." Provide a variety of activities and materials to help develop different motor skills and creative thinking. You might choose a special place in the house where children can play with different media, for example, paint, crayons, stick-on shapes, paper collage, building blocks, ink stamps, and play dough.

Your children's art is always good enough to be in a gallery! Display it. This ultimate compliment will build their self-esteem and encourage further exploration. The display area will also provide an opportunity to talk about ways of *seeing* art rather than looking at it. They'll begin to see art all around them—on buildings, billboards, garden designs, clothing, containers, street signs, menus, and so on. On your visits to the art museum, your children will transfer these seeing skills to "other" famous art on display.

Squeeze It

½ to 1 hour

Painting, drawing, and gluing is fun. But there's nothing easier than to simply squeeze out paint to create art. I hope you've been collecting lots of squeezable plastic bottles. It's time to use them. Caution: don't let your child eat the art.

Supplies

Up to six plastic squeeze bottles
Flour
Salt
Liquid paint
Small mixing bowls
Wooden spoons
Small funnel
Assorted stiff paper

Directions

Mix equal parts of flour and salt in several bowls. Add one color of liquid paint to each bowl and mix ingredients with a spoon to make a paste. Pour each mixture into a squeeze bottle with the help of a funnel. Squeeze paste onto paper, creating a design for a fancy dessert. Let dry. Invent a catchy name for each dessert, for example, "Strawberry Delight Cake."

Extension

Try the same idea with cookie decoration. Use insides of bottle lids instead of paper for the base of the design. Squeeze decorations into the upside down lid. If you have doilies in the house, you can use them as a base, too.

Ex Libris

½ hour +

The Latin word "ex libris" is a term used for a stamp on a book that identifies the book's owner, similar to a logo. Your child will enjoy personalizing his/her collection of books.

Supplies

Inked stamp pad or liquid paint
Small object for carving, e.g., potato, carrot, rubber eraser
Knife
Pencil
Paper

Directions

Discuss the meaning and purpose of an ex libris stamp. Ask your child to design on paper a pictograph symbol of him-or-herself. For example, if the child likes baseball, perhaps a design made up of the child's initials shaped like a baseball would be fun. Help your child carve the design about ⅛" deep on a vegetable or rubber eraser. Test the precision of the cuts from time to time by stamping them on paper. If using poster paints instead of ink from a stamp pad, pour some paint into the lid of a jar or a plastic plate for easy dipping. Your child can stamp the ex libris symbol on the inside cover of books using various colors.

Extension

You may want to play with pictographs. Talk about how pictographs are drawings with a message. They were used by ancient peoples, like Native Americans or Biblical Egyptians, to record events and to send messages. Choose a nursery rhyme or poem. Have your child draw a pictograph for each line or sentence of the text.

Crayon Etchings

¼ hour +

Etching is a wonderful way to see positive/negative space in a different way. The art process happens in reverse to other forms of painting. With painting, you fill up space. When etching, you create space.

Supplies

Several light-colored crayons
One thick black crayon
Blunt scraping tools (for example, bobby pin, paper clip, plastic knife and fork)
Sheet of paper

Directions

Pressing firmly, draw multi-color designs all over the paper using light-colored crayons. Cover the whole design with black crayon. To etch, scrape parts of the black crayon to reveal the colors underneath. Talk about the glow and the texture of the picture.

Extension

Create a greeting card. Fold a sheet of paper into the dimensions of a card. Coat the face of the card heavily with wax crayons. Scratch a design or a message (for example, MOM). Apply glue to some areas of the design and sprinkle tiny objects (for example, glass beads, shredded foil, rice, sequins) onto the glue. Let dry. Brush away pieces that have not adhered to the glue. Write a message inside the card. Give it to a dear friend or you can help your child mail it to a special person.

Cobweb Ball

½ hour on two separate days

This magical ball, seemingly made of air, makes a fanciful decoration for special occasions. You can hang it on the tree at Christmas and make it the centerpiece during a party.

Supplies

Spool of thread
Liquid starch
Small, round balloon

Scissors
String

Directions

Put a spool of thread on its side in a small bowl and cover it completely with liquid starch. Hang a balloon over the bowl. Wind the thread around the balloon. Wind as much thread as needed to create a cobweb. Cut the end of the thread and smooth it down. Let the starch dry overnight. Pop the balloon and remove it gently. Now you can hang the cobweb ball on a tree or a fixture.

Extension

Try making cobwebs in the same manner using inflated square or rectangular plastic bags. As an added touch, make a spider from stovepipe wire or yarn and attach it to the cobweb. Decorate the house with these cobwebs for Halloween.

Bubble Art

½ hour +

"Bubble, bubble, toil and trouble." Be prepared for the water highjinks by placing lots of newspapers in the activity area.

Supplies

Dishwashing soap
Powder paint
Plastic straws

Paper
Small plastic containers

Directions

Spread newsprint on work surface. Mix different powder paints with a small amount of liquid soap in bowls. With a straw, blow one color of liquid until bubbles overflow the rim of the bowl a little. Roll paper around gently on top of the bubbles without bursting or flattening them. Repeat the process with other colors. Let the paper dry. Talk about the bubble effect and the overlapping colors.

Extension

Did you know you can blow bubbles with dishwashing soap? Mix two glasses of soap with six glasses of water, and one to four glasses of glycerine, which you can purchase in any pharmacy. Twist wire into a circle with a handle. Dip the circle into the bowl and blow. With practice, you can blow huge bubbles.

Tablecloth Art

½ to ¾ hour

The next time you have a barbecue, birthday party, or family party, try this simple activity with your children. It's great for fostering creativity—and it's also terrific for keeping your kids happily occupied while you make last-minute preparations.

Supplies

Tables (as many as you plan to use at the party, or one per child)
White paper (either a large roll of paper or a stack of
    continuous-form paper)
Masking tape or other tape that will adhere to the tables
Markers
Pencils

Directions

Cover the table with paper. Tape the paper down so it won't move around. Tell your child that she is going to be in charge of making the tablecloth(s) for the table(s). Discuss what she might like to draw to decorate the tablecloth. Does the party have a theme? Would she like to draw something that incorporates the theme? Is there a guest of honor? Would she like to draw something of particular interest to that guest? Does she know all the guests? Would she like to draw portraits of them? The possibilities are almost endless and the results are invariably more appealing than any store-bought paper table covering.

Extension

You may want to put more time into this activity by planning it beforehand with your child. For example, if the party is a holiday party, a quick trip to the library should yield some good reference material. With your help, your child can learn more about the holiday and plan out an appropriate decoration. Plans do not have to be elaborate—a giant flag for the Fourth of July, a Pilgrim and an Indian for Thanksgiving are challenging enough for this age group. If the party is a birthday party, you may want to help your child plan out some scenes from the birthday person's life.

For example, if Grandpa was a grocer as a young man, a grocery scene would be fun. Again, this activity has almost limitless possibilities. Just let your imagination take hold.

Junior Architect

¼ to ½ hour

This is an easy way to reinforce the skills of creativity and spatial awareness.

Supplies

Large sheet of plain paper (freezer wrap, tagboard, or other papers can be taped together to make one huge sheet about 18″ x 18″ or more)

Ruler

Pencil, crayon, markers

Old magazines, newspapers, catalogs

Scissors

Glue

Directions

Put the paper on the floor and explain to your child that he is going to design his own dream house. It can be for now or something he will live in when he grows up. Let him show you what rooms he wants and where he wants them. Help him outline the spaces with a ruler. Once the rooms are arranged, tell him to cut out pictures and glue them down, until his home is completely "furnished."

Extension

Some children will jump right into this fantasy; others need a little guided imagery. Give a gentle push by telling your child to close his eyes and imagine specific scenarios. For example: "You are in the kitchen. What do you want to eat? Which room do you go to next? What do you see there?" When the house is completed, discuss it with your child. You may get some important insights into his needs and desires.

Paint-a-Cookie

1 to 2 hours

This is an excellent activity for promoting creativity, fine motor development, following directions, and just plain old fun. What makes this cookie project unusual is the use of paintbrushes to apply various colored icings.

Supplies

For the cookies:
- ¾ cup margarine
- ½ cup sifted cornstarch
- ½ cup sifted confectioner's sugar
- 1 cup all-purpose flour
- 1 teaspoon vanilla
- 1 teaspoon almond extract
- Cookie cutters
- Plastic non-sharp knives

For the icing:
- 1 cup confectioner's sugar
- Water
- Food coloring
- Clean, new paintbrushes or pastry brushes

Directions

Help your child make the cookies by following these simple directions: Cream margarine and add dry ingredients, one at a time. Add extracts and mix well, forming into a ball of dough. Refrigerate for a few hours and then roll out on a floured surface (dough should be about ¼" thick). Use cookie cutters or plastic knives to cut cookie shapes. Place cookies on a greased cookie sheet and bake at 350 degrees for approximately eight to ten minutes or until golden brown. Cool cookies completely before using the icing "paint." (Note: This recipe makes between 24 and 36 cookies depending on the size of your cutters.)

For the icing, mix confectioner's sugar and water until the icing is the consistency of slightly diluted sour cream. Divide icing into smaller batches and use food coloring to make several different colors of icing "paint." Put a clean paintbrush into each cup of icing and allow children to paint their cookies any way they like. Leave plenty of time for this part of the activity; some children will work on this project for an hour or more.

Extension

Provide your child with sprinkles and other edible ornaments to enhance his cookie painting. If you prefer, instead of making many individual cookies, your child could also make one giant cookie which could be painted as a scene.

Bath Beautification

½ hour +

This activity will give your child experience with measurement, counting, and following directions. When it's over, he'll have a set of bathtub crayons that can be safely used on your bathtub tiles in many creative learning projects.

Supplies

Water
Measuring cup that can measure quantities in ⅛ cup increments
Ivory Snowflakes
Food coloring in assorted colors
Ice cube molds or miniature muffin tins

Directions

Help your child follow these directions for making soap crayons. Measure out ⅛ cup of water. Measure ⅛ cup of Ivory Snowflakes. Combine ingredients. Divide into two batches. Add 15–25 drops of food coloring to each batch. Pour mixture into ice cube molds or muffin tin molds. Allow to harden and dry (this may take a few days). Pop "crayons" out of the molds and start writing!

Extension

Bath time can be one of the calmest times of the day with these do-it-yourself bath crayons. Use them to teach the alphabet, letter sounds, and so on. Almost anything is more fun to learn when the teaching's done in the bathtub.

She Saves Seashells

½ hour +

Most children love to collect seashells, but not many make the most of them. By exercising imagination and manual dexterity, a child can create something truly special.

Supplies

Shells

Pot of water

Newspaper

Q-tips, tweezers

Shellac

Brushes

Cardboard

Glue

Directions

Help your child to carefully check her shells and make sure there is nothing living inside them! Boil the shells (with your child at a safe distance) and, when they are cool, have your child use the Q-Tips or tweezers to thoroughly clean them. Now she can wash the shells in warm soapy water in a sink. When the shells are dry, she can paint them with one or two coats of shellac. Tell her to arrange the shells on the cardboard to make a picture. The picture can be abstract or realistic as she pleases. Help her to see what objects the shapes suggest, for example some shells may resemble fans, while others might resemble faces or purses. Your child can save the picture by gluing the shells onto the cardboard.

Extension

There are many creative ways to use shells. Your child can draw large outlines of her initials on the cardboard and fill them in with the shells. If the shells have holes in them, she can make a necklace or bracelet with a needle and thread. She can use glue, buttons, and poster paint to make silly shell animals.

Sponge Printing

¼ to ½ hour

Sponge printing is versatile and simple enough for the very young to manage with only a little assistance. Sponge prints are wonderful for holiday and birthday cards. This activity will introduce your child to a new art technique and stimulate creativity.

Supplies

Flat sponges
Felt tip markers
Scissors
Poster and paint and paintbrush
Paper plate
Paper

Directions

With felt tip marker, draw a simple design on sponge. Cut it out. Then pour some paint onto a paper plate. Dip sponge into paint. Press paint-filled sponge onto white paper—you have a sponge print! (You'll have to do some experimentation for best results. Try different amounts of paint on the sponge until the result is what you want.)

Extension

Use sponge painting for holidays and birthday celebrations. Ask your child to think about what design Grandpa would like, or a favorite cousin, or his friend, and you're on your way.

Consider also talking about other forms of printing with your child. A "relief" print—in which all the raised or relief portions are printed—can be made with a potato. Slice a potato in half. Cut a simple pattern on its surface, and then paint the potato surface with tempura paint. Apply painted potato print to paper and you've created a relief print, potato fashion.

Soap on a Rope

½ hour

Some kids see bath time as a chance to splash about, but not necessarily soap up. These kids are good candidates for handmade "soap on a rope." It's one art project that has the side benefit of making bath time more attractive.

Supplies

> Slivers of soap you have saved
> Double boiler
> Wooden spoon
> Juice can or muffin tin
> Heavy yarn

Directions

Save bits and pieces of soap, the more colors the merrier. Once you have accumulated a good supply, put the soap in the top part of a double boiler and fill bottom part two-thirds full with water. Bring double boiler to a boil and then reduce heat to a simmer. Stir soap until melted. (This stove work will require very careful supervision, perhaps even intervention, on the part of parents.) When melted, pour liquid into your juice can "mold" or the muffin tin. Do *not* allow your child to pour the very hot soap. As the soap cools and congeals, insert two ends of folded 22" yarn into soap, leaving loop end out. When soap hardens, tap out of mold with warm water. Soap on a rope!

Extension

In our disposable world, soap on a rope is a good lesson in recycling. Talk to your kids about recycling and why it is important. If your neighborhood has a recycling project, get involved and get your kids involved. Save those newspapers and soda cans, and perhaps even propose neighborhood cleanups that recycle roadside cans and the like.

You may also want to explain to your child that before people used soap they washed themselves with olive oil, plant ashes, pumice stones, or sand. Colonial Americans (among others) made their own soap out of household fats and greases. This process was quite time-consuming. Does your child think he'd like to spend a lot of time making his own soap? Or washing clothes without a washing machine?

Play Clay

½ hour

Many a rainy day can be brightened by a lump of colored clay and a good imagination. This recipe for play clay is inexpensive and easy to make. Have your child help you measure out the ingredients and follow the directions—both of these are important skills for school success.

Supplies

1 ½ cups flour
½ cup salt
½ cup water
¼ cup vegetable oil
Food coloring

Directions

Mix together salt and flour. Slowly add vegetable oil and water. Add one or two drops of food coloring. (If you want to make assorted colors, divide the clay or increase the recipe.) Knead clay until completely mixed. If you find the clay is too sticky, add more flour. Store in a sealed plastic container. Some people find the clay lasts longer if it's kept in the refrigerator.

For enduring works of art, allow projects to harden in the air for two or three days. Another option is to bake the project for a couple of hours in a 250 degree oven. When hard, coat the project with white craft glue. After the glue has dried, the project may be colored with markers or watercolor paints.

Extension

Sometimes children want to make something but just can't think of an idea. Rather than simply supplying an idea, consider this alternative: choose a colorful picture book that features some interesting human or animal characters. Read the story to your child and suggest that he make one of the animals or characters from the book.

Rainy Day Scrapbook

½ to 1 hour

Not much imagination goes into a sticker scrapbook. It is a prepackaged, instant hobby. But the old-fashioned picture scrapbook is another matter. Provide your child with a stack of old magazines and suggest some possible subjects to collect (anything from faces to flowers). Soon he will be totally absorbed in a hobby that can bring him pleasure for years.

Supplies

Scrapbook
Scissors
Stack of old magazines
White craft glue

Directions

Talk over with your child how he wants to organize his scrapbook. He may want to combine many things in one book, filling a page with flowers, another page with eyeglasses, another with faces, and so on. Once he has made some initial choices, give him a stack of old magazines.

Each time he finds an appropriate picture, he can cut it out and paste it into his scrapbook. Slowly, his skill with scissors will improve, along with his design sense. If he's ready to write, you might also consider helping him to write captions for his pictures.

Extension

Children have great fun learning their ABCs with a scrapbook. As pages fill up with pictures that begin with each letter of the alphabet, their letter skills grow. The same is true for their number skills when a scrapbook is organized around objects from one to ten.

Stamp Treasure Box

½ to 1 hour

A kindergarten-age child is not quite ready for a stamp collection. But chances are he'll jump at the chance to create a stamp treasure box. It's an artistic way to introduce the many worlds of stamps: from nature's kingdom to history and art.

Supplies

Collection of stamps
Cigar box
White craft glue
Tweezers

Directions

Before beginning this project, you will need to amass a collection of stamps. Your family mail, friends, and the work place will all provide you with stamps. Once soaked in water for ten minutes, the stamps will come loose from their envelopes. Then they can be left to dry on a towel. (Let your child do all the preparation. He'll enjoy it.) The next step is to glue the stamps onto the cigar box. The tweezers help in picking up the stamps. Be sure to cover the entire top and sides so that a colorful allover pattern emerges. The box makes a great gift or your child may use it for his own collection—perhaps of stamps!

Extension

Almost every stamp you look at has a story to tell. You can use stamps to introduce your child to geography, history, art, botany, and much more. Let his own interests be your guide. If you find he is especially interested in flower stamps, for example, then why not see if you can learn about some of the flowers pictured on your stamps and even identify them at a nearby botanical garden? Or if famous people seem to interest him, now is a good time to start learning about past presidents and other historical figures. The history of stamps, and how our post office works, are other areas to pursue.

Snowscaping

¼ to ¾ hour

Here's a way to stimulate your child's shaving cream show-manship and clean your windows at the same time. You may discover an artist in the making.

Supplies

    Shaving cream
    Paper towels

Directions

Have your child squirt shaving cream on a large window or sliding glass door. Using her fingers, allow her to smooth the cream and fingerpaint in it. Can she draw a snowman? How about snowflakes and icicles? The sky's the limit with this delightful, gushy "paint."

When your artist is tired of creating, let the cream dry and wipe it off with a paper towel. Your windows will sparkle!

Extension

Have your child use her shaving cream easel to practice writing her letters or numbers. How about tic-tac-toe on the window? Even math problems are fun when they're done by fingertip on shaving-cream-covered windows.

Holiday Magnets

½ to 1 hour

The only limit to holiday magnets is your child's imagination. From a menorah and dreidel to Santa and his reindeer, all seasons and faiths can be included. This fun activity will encourage your child's creativity and help him hone his fine motor skills.

Supplies

Pencil and paper
Scissors
Felt scraps in assorted colors
Felt tip pen
White craft glue
Glitter
Magnetic sheet (available at craft stores)

Directions

Make a list of the holidays your family likes to celebrate. Then have your child draw symbols of these holidays with pencil and paper. He may wish, for example, to draw a dreidel for Chanukah, a heart for Valentine's Day, and a flag for the Fourth of July. Once he is happy with his design, he should use it as a pattern for this felt cutout. The cutout can be decorated with the felt tip pen, some glitter, and other colored scraps of felt. Once the cutout is complete, glue it to an appropriately sized piece of the magnetic sheet. Now your holiday magnet is ready for the refrigerator door.

Extension

Holiday magnets are not only fun to make, they're also ways

to enrich the holidays by understanding them better. Make a point of reading at least one book together about whatever holiday your magnet commemorates. Then delve into mysteries: Why does the American flag have stars and stripes on it? Why does the menorah burn for eight nights? Who was St. Patrick? The next thing you know, your child will be bringing his knowledge, and the magnets, to nursery school—another place where holidays are studied.